Beginning WatchKit Development

Cory Bohon
Kyle Richter

I would like to dedicate this book to my parents and to my mentors who have taught and helped me achieve things that would not have been possible without them.
— *Cory Bohon*

I dedicate this book to my middle school English teacher who told me I didn't know how to write and to my guidance counselor who said I would never amount to anything.
— *Kyle Richter*

Table of Contents

PREFACE	8
PREREQUISITES	8
WHAT YOU'LL NEED	8
ABOUT THE SAMPLE CODE a.k.a WHY NOT SWIFT	9
GETTING SAMPLE CODE	10
INSTALLING GIT AND WORKING WITH GITHUB	10
CONTACTING THE AUTHORS	10
ACKNOWLEDGEMENTS	11
ABOUT THE AUTHORS	12
CHAPTER 1: INTRODUCTION TO THE APPLE WATCH	16
INTRODUCTION	16
A BRIEF HISTORY OF THE WATCH	17
APPLE WATCH	18
WATCHKIT	20
TYPES OF WATCH APPS	21
CHAPTER 2: TESTING ON DEVICES AND THE SIMULATOR	24
THE SIMULATOR	24
BUILDING FOR THE SIMULATOR	25
BUILDING FOR THE DEVICE	26
CHAPTER 3: DESIGNING FOR APPLE WATCH	30
ICON DESIGN	31
DESIGNING IMAGE ASSETS	34
USING THE IMAGE CACHE	37
COLOR	39
TYPOGRAPHY	41
CHAPTER 4: ADVANCED WATCHKIT CONTROLS	44
TABLE	46
PICKER	52
MAP	57

CHAPTER 5: WATCHKIT MULTIMEDIA — 64

- INTRODUCTION TO VIDEO PLAYBACK IN WATCHOS — 64
- ENCODING — 65
- PLAYING AUDIO AND VIDEO WITH WKINTERFACEMOVIE — 66
- PRESENTING THE MEDIA CONTROLLER PROGRAMMATICALLY — 71
- RECORDING AUDIO WITH BUILT-IN MICROPHONE — 73
- AUDIO PLAYBACK — 76
- HAPTIC FEEDBACK AND SOUNDS — 79

CHAPTER 6: THE WATCH CONNECTIVITY FRAMEWORK — 82

- SETTING UP A WCSESSION CONNECTION — 83
- UNDERSTANDING THE SESSION STATE — 85
- WATCH CONNECTIVITY FRAMEWORK COMMUNICATION CATEGORIES — 86
- IMPLEMENTING BACKGROUND TRANSFERS — 88
- IMPLEMENTING INTERACTIVE MESSAGING — 97
- NSURLSESSION — 101

CHAPTER 7: BUILDING COMPLICATIONS WITH CLOCKKIT — 104

- HOW COMPLICATIONS WORK — 104
- DESIGN CONSIDERATIONS FOR COMPLICATIONS — 105
- CONFIGURING A PROJECT FOR COMPLICATIONS — 111
- IMPLEMENTING A COMPLICATION — 113
- ABOUT TEXT AND IMAGE PROVIDERS — 121
- HANDLING UPDATES TO DATA — 122

CHAPTER 8: ACCESSING THE SENSORS — 126

- ACCESSING DEVICE SENSORS — 126
- ACCESSING HEART RATE DATA — 132
- HEALTHKIT SUBMISSION REQUIREMENTS — 138

CHAPTER 9: ANIMATION TECHNIQUES — 140

- SIZING METHODS — 140
- ANIMATING CHANGES TO WKINTERFACEOBJECTS — 142
- ANIMATION TIPS — 143
- ANIMATING CHANGES TO WKINTERFACETABLE — 144

CHAPTER 10: ALERTS — 148

- ALERTS AND ACTION SHEETS — 148
- IMPLEMENTING AN ALERT — 150

CHAPTER 11: USER INPUT AND INTERNATIONALIZATION — 154

- ABOUT USER INPUT ON APPLE WATCH — 154
- CAPTURING USER INPUT — 155
- INTERNATIONALIZATION — 158

CHAPTER 12: HANDOFF — 162

- HOW HANDOFF WORKS — 163
- REGISTERING ACTIVITIES — 164
- BROADCASTING APP-BASED ACTIVITIES — 165
- THE willDisappear METHOD AND CALL invalidateUserActivity. — 166
- HANDLING AND RESUMING ACTIVITIES — 167
- BROADCASTING WEB-BASED ACTIVITIES — 169

CHAPTER 13: BUILDING DOCK-COMPATIBLE WATCHOS APPS — 172

- ABOUT THE DOCK — 172
- MAKING APPS DOCKABLE — 173
- MAKING NEW SNAPSHOTS — 174

CHAPTER 14: DISTRIBUTING WATCHKIT APPS — 180

- iOS PROVISIONING — 180
- BUILD NUMBERS — 183
- GENERATING AN ARCHIVE BUILD — 184
- CREATE AND UPLOAD AN IPA TO iTUNES CONNECT — 185
- iTUNES CONNECT REQUIRED ASSETS — 187
- AUTOMATICALLY INCREMENTING BUILD NUMBERS IN XCODE — 188

APPENDIX I: BUILDING THE SAMPLE APP — 192

- XCODE VERSION REQUIRED FOR WATCHKIT DEVELOPMENT — 192
- CREATING THE SAMPLE PROJECT — 192
- WRITING THE NETWORKING CODE — 193
- CREATING THE MASTER-DETAIL VIEW CONTROLLERS — 200
- CREATING THE WATCHKIT APP TARGET — 206
- HELLO, WATCHKIT — 207

Preface

Welcome to *Beginning WatchKit Development!*

The following chapters will walk the reader through the process of building a complete Apple Watch app with an accompanying iOS app. This publication aims to provide development information on a beginner level for existing iOS developers to quickly get up and running building apps for the Apple Watch.

Early chapters cover the basics, from a brief history of WatchKit development, to testing and working with the simulator, to designing apps for a niche device. Throughout the course of the publication, all aspects of watch development will be covered in depth, including working with WatchKit Controls, Connectivity, Multimedia, Complications, Sensors, and more. After finishing this publication, readers will be well equipped to build a variety of both simple and complex watch apps.

Prerequisites

While every effort has been made to keep this book at the beginner level it would greatly benefit the reader to have a cursory knowledge of not only software development but also iOS development. This includes knowledge of C, Objective-C, Swift, Xcode, and Interface Builder.

What You'll Need

Although you can develop Apple Watch apps in the simulator, it is recommended that you have at least one iOS device and an Apple Watch available for testing. In addition you will need the following:

1) Apple Developer Account: The latest version of the iOS developer tools – including Xcode and the iOS SDKs/WatchKit SDK – can be

downloaded for free from Apple's Developer Portal (http://developer.apple.com/ios). To ship an app to the App Store or to install and test on a personal device, you will also need a paid developer account at $99 per year.

2) Macintosh Computer: To develop for iOS and Apple Watch, and to run Xcode, you will need a modern Mac computer capable of running the latest release of macOS.

3) Internet Connection: Many features of WatchKit development require a constant Internet connection for your Mac as well as for the device you are building against.

About the Sample Code a.k.a Why not Swift

The sample code for *Beginning WatchKit Development* appears in written form throughout the following pages in Objective-C. When we first set out to write this book a lot of thought and consideration went into selecting the "primary" book language. We decide it did not make sense to present both languages for each example, and at this time Swift is still experiencing frequent changes. In addition, we found that although most of our readers knew both languages, those who knew only one were familiar with Objective-C.

For the convenience of the reader, however, the downloadable sample code that accompanies this book is made available in both Objective-C and Swift. Throughout the writing process we put great effort into ensuring that the code samples were simple, easy to follow, and as language-independent as possible. We understand that there are two very different schools of thought when it comes to picking a language for modern Apple platform development, we hope that we have been able to provide a reasonable middle ground for everyone.

Getting Sample Code

The sample code for *Beginning WatchKit Development* can be viewed, downloaded, or cloned on GitHub at the following URL:

https://github.com/corybohon/BeginningWatchKitDevelopment

Installing Git and Working with Github

Git is one of the most popular version control systems. To clone or make a copy of the source code found on GitHub, you will first need to install Git on your Mac. A command-line version of Git is included in the Xcode command-line tool installation. Alternately, a current installer for Git can be found at http://git-scm.com/downloads. There are several GUI apps for Git, which may be more appealing to some developers. If you prefer not to install Git, GitHub also allows for downloading the source files in the form of a compressed zip file.

GitHub provides free basic accounts that can be set up at https://github.com/signup/free. After Git has been installed, you may download a copy of the sample code into the current working directory from the terminal's command line by typing

```
$git clone git@github.com/corybohon/BeginningWatchKitDevelopment
```

and then hitting enter.

Contacting the Authors

The authors can be contacted through watchkitbook.com or by emailing authors@watchkitbook.com. We encourage everyone to send us feedback, corrections, and errors. Feedback is extremely helpful in not only letting us know what people like, but also what they did not care for. This will allow us to ensure future editions are as error-free and as useful as possible to our readers.

Acknowledgements

This book could not have existed without a great deal of effort from far too many behind-the-scenes people; although there are only two authors on the cover, dozens of people were responsible for bringing this book to completion.

We would also like to thank Momo Yang for lending her talent to help bring the cover art to life. We would also like to thank George Williams for his long hours of copyediting and effort in helping us find the perfect words to explain what was inside our own heads. We would also like to acknowledge and thank Beau G. Bolle for taking the time out of his busy schedule to provide technical feedback and corrections. We would also like to acknowledge all those who provided feedback for us throughout the process especially Eric Blair for his insightful notes on the first draft.

A special thanks is also due for Justin Williams who took the time to write the foreword.

Writing a book occupies a considerable amount of time that was shouldered not only by us but also by our families and co-workers. We would like to thank everyone who surrounds us in our daily lives for taking a considerable amount of work off of our plates, as well as understanding the demands that a project like this brings.

Finally, we would like to thank the community at large. Quite often we consulted developer forums, blog posts, and associates to ask questions or provide feedback. Without the hard efforts of everyone in the iOS community, this book would not be nearly as complete.

About the Authors

Cory Bohon is a Cross Platform Engineer at MartianCraft, working on a daily basis with quality-discerning clients like Apple, Whole Foods, FOX, Lytro, and with internal products at MartianCraft. He is also the owner of Cocoa App, a software company that creates niche productivity and utility apps for Apple platforms. Cory fell in love with computers at an early age, and began writing software for the Mac while in high school. His early software garnered more than a half a million downloads in only a few months, and earned the recognition of podcasters and bloggers. Since 2008, Cory has been crafting software full time for Apple-only platforms, beginning with the introduction of the iPhone SDK. He calls South Carolina home, and when not writing code, he enjoys spending time collecting old Apple gear, traveling, and being an amateur photographer. He can be found on Twitter @coryb.

Kyle Richter is the Chief Executive Officer and Founder at MartianCraft, a twice-named Inc 5000 fastest growing startup. Kyle began developing software in the early 1990s and has always been dedicated to the Apple ecosystem. He has authored and coauthored several books on iOS development, including *Beginning iOS Game Center Development, Beginning Social Game Development, iOS Components and Frameworks,* and *Mastering iOS Frameworks.* Between running day-to-day operations at MartianCraft, Kyle travels the world speaking on development, entrepreneurship, and futurology. He currently calls Washington DC home, where he spends his time with his border collie. He can be found on Twitter @kylerichter.

Foreward

Written by Justin Williams

I first started working with Apple platforms back in 2001. This was at the height of the transition from Classic MacOS to Mac OS X. Not only was the operating system in flux, but so was the development platform Apple developers would need to learn to build best-of-breed Mac OS X apps.

In 2001 there was a single book on Mac OS X, Objective-C, and the Cocoa frameworks. Fast-forward fifteen years later and Apple is one of the largest companies in the world with many of the most popular development platforms today. There's not just one book, but dozens of books and other learning resources to choose from. The iPhone ushered in much of this change in perception and popularity for Apple, and its success has bred new platforms to extend your iOS and macOS knowledge to.

When Apple Watch was first introduced in the fall of 2014 it was touted as the most intimate product the company has ever produced. This intimacy extends beyond just being close to the skin of its users. watchOS apps need to be quick, glanceable, and most important performant. While there are many similarities between iOS and watchOS, the key differences and how you tackle them are what will separate a good watchOS app from a great one.

Cory and Kyle have written a book that serves not only as an excellent introduction to watchOS development for the beginning mobile developer, but also an excellent ramp onboard the WatchKit frameworks for seasoned iOS or macOS developers.

I approached "Beginning WatchKit Development" as someone with over 15 years experience as an Apple developer, but zero experience with the Watch outside of wearing one on my wrist every day for the 18 months. I came away with the knowledge and knowhow to build my first great watchOS app.

Like Apple Watch itself, Cory and Kyle's book is approachable, easy to understand, and fun to read and learn from. Unlike Apple Watch, it is thankfully not intimate.

About Justin Williams
Justin Williams is a macOS and iOS developer located in sunny Denver, Colorado. He currently leading a merry band of mobile development misfits at TED.

Chapter 1: Introduction to The Apple Watch

Chapter Overview

The Apple Watch, first introduced to the world September 2014, ushered in a new era of wearable smart devices. This chapter will introduce the Apple Watch as well as WatchKit, the SDK for developing native software.

These topics will be covered in this chapter:

- An introduction to smart watches
- A brief history of wrist watches
- The Apple Watch
- WatchKit SDK
- The types of watch apps developers can write

Introduction

From Dick Tracy and James Bond to Knight Rider and even Turanga Leela, dreams of the impending techno-future have overflowed with wearable smart devices. For generations, science fiction fans have dreamed of futuristic technology strapped to their wrist.

The Apple Watch is by no means the first smart watch available, just as the iPod wasn't the first MP3 player, the iMac wasn't the first personal computer, and the iPhone wasn't the first smart phone. However, all of these devices went on to redefine their respective industries. And while it's still too early to say whether smart watches will change the world, the Apple Watch is a very young device with unbounded potential. It will continue to evolve with the help and dedication of third party developers.

A Brief History of the Watch

Just as understanding the history of the personal computer is valuable when writing desktop software, understanding the origins of the wristwatch will prove useful when developing software for the wearable world.

World War I brought with it the first need for precision military coordination; during this first modern war, soldiers began strapping pocket watches – which had existed since the sixteenth century – onto their wrists, quickly providing access to the time. By the summer of 1916 the *New York Times* expressed bewilderment at the rapidly increasing trend of wearing watches on wrists. The Times quipped "the bracelet watch has been looked upon by Americans as more or less of a joke. Vaudeville artists and moving-picture actors have utilized it as a funmaker, as a 'silly ass' fad." The world was changing, as everything began to happen in quicker succession, having access to the current time was becoming a necessity for all walks of life.

Early watches required users to wind them frequently, but self-winding watches, which still remain popular today, soon replaced these. Introduced in the late 1950's Quartz watches started to dominate the market by the 1970's. Quartz watches drastically reduced the price while increasing the accuracy of modern watches. Most analog watches today are Quartz driven, given away by their telltale tick once a second. Automatic or mechanical watches still remain popular today with the higher end market and brands such as Rolex, Omega, and Seiko remain household names.

A blurry line exists between digital watches and smart watches; there is no clear first smart watch. Without a doubt, Apple Watch cannot be called the first smart watch. Like the iPod, iPhone, and iMac, it was preceded by numerous rivals. It remains to be seen if the Apple Watch can capture the same spirit and become the device against which all others are measured.

Apple Watch

Rumors about a possible Apple Watch had existed for nearly a decade before the announcement of the device in September 2014. The Apple Watch is widely regarded as the first major project of then newly-named Apple CEO Tim Cook. The device quickly became the best-selling wearable technology with sales exceeding 12 million units in the first year it was available.

While the Apple Watch comes in two generations and three "editions" – Sport, Watch/Standard, Edition – the differences among these are entirely cosmetic and will not affect the development or deployment of apps. Each edition of the Apple Watch is available in two screen sizes, 38 mm and 42 mm. Traditionally, watch size is measured bezel to bezel and range in size from 18 mm to 68 mm. The Apple Watch, however, is measured diagonally the same as a typical computer monitor, and like a monitor it does not include the bezel (Figure 1-1). The screen resolution differs slightly between the two physical sizes, with the 38 mm boasting a 272x340 resolution and the 42 mm features a 312x390 resolution.

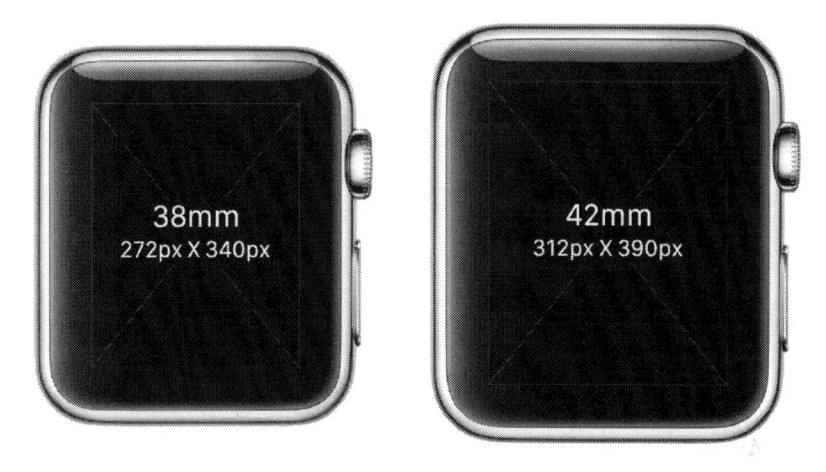

Figure 1.1 – The screen and bezel sizes for the two available Apple Watches.

The Apple Watch features a bidirectional hardware crown — a term borrowed from mechanical watches — for scrolling and selecting, a power button, and a Force Touch-capable screen. The Apple watch also features an array of sensors both external (Figure 1-2) and internal. The rear sensors include infrared and visible-light LEDS in addition to photo sensors, which all work in unison to detect the user's heart rate. These sensors are also used to determine if the device has been removed from the user's wrist since last authenticating. Internally, the Apple Watch features an accelerometer to detect motion and a linear actuator that provides haptic feedback, which Apple calls the "Taptic Engine."

Figure 1.2 – Four sensors found on the rear of the Apple Watch used for detecting the user's heart rate.

WatchKit

Macs and iOS devices have their own SDKs. Apple Watch is no different, and WatchKit is the framework that powers it. WatchKit is a powerful set of frameworks largely derived from UIKIt. Developers who have a background in iOS development will feel right at home with WatchKit objects like `WKInterfaceLabel` and `WKInterfaceButton`. Despite having many similarities to iOS, WatchKit is designed to be used on a smaller and more specialized device.

Every Apple Watch app consists of three unique components:

- **A Containing App** on a paired iOS device, which is used to install the watch app onto the device.
- **A WatchKit App on the watch**, which contains all the user interface elements.

- **A WatchKit Extension**, which will contain the code for the watch app. In version 1.0 of WatchOS, the WatchKit Extension was hosted on the iOS device. Starting in version 2.0, the WatchKit Extension is executed on the watch itself.

Types of Watch Apps

There are three different feature areas on the watch where watch apps can be deployed by a third party developer; each has a specialized purpose and design:

- **WatchKit Apps**, the most traditional type of app, are fully functional, live on the Apple Watch, and can interact with the iOS parent app.
- **Notifications**, displayed messages from the paired iOS app, can be spawned both locally and remotely.
- **Complications**, a term borrowed from traditional watches, add small areas of detail to the watch face such as a calendar, moon cycle, or weather.

Summary

This chapter introduced the very basics of WatchKit and provided a foundation for understanding the development, terminology, and principles of Apple Watch development. Additionally, a brief history of watches and smart watches was provided. You should feel comfortable with the Apple Watch itself and the general terminology and functionality to begin moving into development.

Going Further

Like many modern technological developments, the Apple Watch – and by extension the smart watch – share a rich history with physical devices that have been a part of our society for a long time. The more you understand about the role, functions, and spirit of traditional mechanical watches, the more you will understand the driving forces behind smart watches. Take some time to learn more about the history of the wrist watch and some of the major changes that took place over the last century.

Chapter 2: Testing on Devices and the Simulator

Chapter Overview

Professionals know that testing their work is of the utmost importance; of course, software development is no exception. Tremendous effort has been made to ensure that Apple Watch apps are easy to test and debug, which is no small feat considering the multitude of challenges that surround wearable devices.

The following material demonstrates the process of testing watch apps not only on physical hardware but on the iOS simulator to imitate the unique input features found on the watch. While the iOS simulator provides a very advanced test platform, the importance of testing any software on the actual product it is intended to run on cannot be overstated.

The Simulator

Developers familiar with iPhone, iPad, or Apple TV development will feel right at home when it comes to building and debugging on the Apple Watch. The same tools are shared across all of Apple's development environments.

The Apple Watch has several special input methods not found on the Mac as well as some unique to the watch not even being available on other mobile devices. Simulating Force Touch input and interacting with the digital crown are important tools for building a fully functional and intuitive watch app. Figure 2.1 demonstrates how to replicate the distinct behaviors found on the watch using a Mac.

Watch Input	Desktop Input
Single Tap	Mouse Click
Double-Tap	Mouse Double Click
Shallow Force Touch Press	Choose Hardware > Touch Pressure > Shallow Press OR CMD+Shift+1
Deep Force Touch Press	Choose Hardware > Touch Pressure > Deep Press OR CMD+Shift+2
Twist the crown clockwise	Drag up on watch interface
Twist the crown counterclockwise	Drag down on watch interface
Twist the crown quickly	Quick Drag

Figure 2.1 – Simulator input equivalents for the Apple Watch.

Building for the Simulator

Every Apple Watch app is built on top of a companion iOS app. Once a new WatchKit target has been created in a new or existing project it can be built and run. Building to the simulator for the first time will launch the iOS simulator as well as the Apple Watch simulator, which should show a black screen with the current time and a charging icon.

If the WatchKit app employs notifications it may be necessary to test and debug these while working within the simulator. When selecting a new watch target and checking the Notifications checkbox during setup, Xcode will create a new template

PushNotificationPayload.apns file inside of the project (Figure 2-2). When selecting to run a notification interface scheme, Xcode will add a menu for choosing one of the payload files.

This PushNotificationPayload.apns contains static content to simulate a push notification. When running the notification scheme, the notification interface from the Storyboard will display in the simulator with the push contents from the apns file. This is not, however, a replacement for testing push notifications on an actual device because it does not route a notification through the standard delegate methods.

```
{
    "aps": {
        "alert": "Test message content",
        "title": "Optional title",
        "category": "myCategory"
    },

    "WatchKit Simulator Actions": [
        {
            "title": "First Button",
            "identifier": "firstButtonAction"
        }
    ],

    "customKey": "Use this file to define a testing payload for your
        notifications. The aps dictionary specifies the category, alert text and
        title. The WatchKit Simulator Actions array can provide info for one or
        more action buttons in addition to the standard Dismiss button. Any other
        top level keys are custom payload. If you have multiple such JSON files in
        your project, you'll be able to select them when choosing to debug the
        notification interface of your Watch App."
}
```

Figure 2.2 – The default PushNotificationPayload.apns

Building for the Device

Running a watch app on an Apple Watch differs slightly from the typical procedure found with other devices. In order to debug on hardware, both an Apple Watch as well as a compatible iPhone are required, and both must be set up as development devices. First the Apple Watch needs to be paired through the "Watch" app on the iPhone.

Once the devices have been paired together, testing on the Apple Watch is done by installing the new software through the iPhone. It may be required from time to time to remove an installed app from the device; this can be done by accessing the "Devices" option under Window inside of Xcode.

If the Apple Watch and iPhone are provisioned through an Apple Developer account, it is also possible to debug directly on the Apple Watch over the air. To do this, ensure the iPhone is connected to the Mac running Xcode and the Apple Watch is charged, paired, and unlocked. Next, select the scheme to run in the Xcode window and select the test device from the target device list. Building and running will cause the iOS app to be installed on the iPhone, followed by the watchOS app on the Apple Watch. After a few seconds (or a few minutes, depending on app size) the watchOS app will launch and Xcode will be able to debug the app.

Summary

The importance of thoroughly testing software on the devices for which it is intended cannot be overstated. Since the introduction of iPhone development, Xcode has always provided incredible simulator tools to make debugging as quick and painless as possible. This chapter covered both of those technologies and has laid the groundwork to dive headfirst into Apple Watch Development.

Going Further

Debugging and testing mobile software has always been challenging, doubly so for wearable technology. Having a firm grasp of the process and behavior of deploying and debugging watch apps will provide a leg up while learning WatchKit development. Before a project becomes more complicated, try debugging and running under several different scenarios until it feels like second nature.

Chapter 3: Designing for Apple Watch

Chapter Overview

Apple Watch apps have a specific and unique design, especially when compared to iOS apps. The user interface is designed to provide users with a great experience on a small screen while maximizing battery life. The abundance of black backgrounds is no accident; the active-matrix organic light-emitting diode (AMOLED) screen is designed in a way that black colors use less battery life than brighter colors. This is just one example of design choices on the watch intended to extend battery life.

In this chapter the following topics related to watch app design are covered:

- How to design, format, and implement Apple Watch icons
- How to design standard assets for use in watch apps
- How to understand typography on the Apple Watch
- How to leverage color in watch apps
- How to use the image cache and Xcode Assets to store images for use in apps
- How to use the Apple Watch image cache to store frequently utilized images

It's important to note that with Apple Watch design icons and other images created specifically for use with the watch do not require @1x versions because all versions of the watch featuring Retina screens.

Icon Design

Apple Watch apps have a specific icon design unique to the platform. The rounded icons used throughout the system make colors stand out against the black background, which makes for easy tap targets.

The watch icon will be displayed in several locations, requiring the creation of separate varying sizes of the icon.

The first location the icon will be displayed is inside the Watch app located on the connected iPhone. Since the watch is compatible with the iPhone 5 and above, only Retina icons will need to be generated. An additional @3x resolution icon is required for iPhone Plus-size devices.

The second location where the icon will be displayed is within the Apple Watch notification system. Three versions of the icon are needed: a large version for the short look notification, a medium version for the long look notification, and a small version to be displayed in the Notification Center that provides the history of previous notifications.

Since the Apple Watch comes in two screen sizes – the 38mm and the 42mm – two versions of each of the icons are needed. Figure 3.1 provides an overview of the sizes and filenames for the icons.

Asset Filename	Asset Use Case	Asset Size in Pixels
AppIcon29x29@2x.png	Watch Companion App	56 x 56
AppIcon29x29@3x.png	Watch Companion App	87 x 87
AppIcon27.5x27.5@2x.png	Notification Center icon (42mm)	55 x 55
AppIcon24x24@2x.png	Notification Center icon (38mm)	48 x 48
AppIcon44x44@2x.png	Long-Look notification icon and Home Screen (42mm)	88 x 88
AppIcon40x40@2x.png	Long-Look notification icon and Home Screen (38mm)	80 x 80
AppIcon98x98@2x.png	Short-Look icon (42mm)	196 x 196
AppIcon86x86@2x.png	Short-Look icon (38mm)	172 x 172

Figure 3.1 – The formatted filenames for the watch app icons, the use cases, and the Retina size (in pixels) for the icons.

When creating watch icons, do not add any rounded corners to the assets: the rounded corners will be masked automatically. The entire image should be a full-square bleed. If the icon contains a white background, watchOS will add a small, dark gray stroke around the outline of the icon to help it stand out.

When processing assets, use a standard bit-depth of 24 bits – 8 bits each for red, green, and blue – without an alpha channel. Finally, when exporting the icons, use PNG files for all icons and avoid using interlaced PNGs.

After creating these icon versions, place them into the WatchKit project by opening the "Assets.xcassets" file inside the "WatchKit App" folder. Placeholders will already exist for the watch icons under the "AppIcon" image set. Drag and drop the appropriately sized icons into their designated spots to be included in the compiled binary (Figure 3.2).

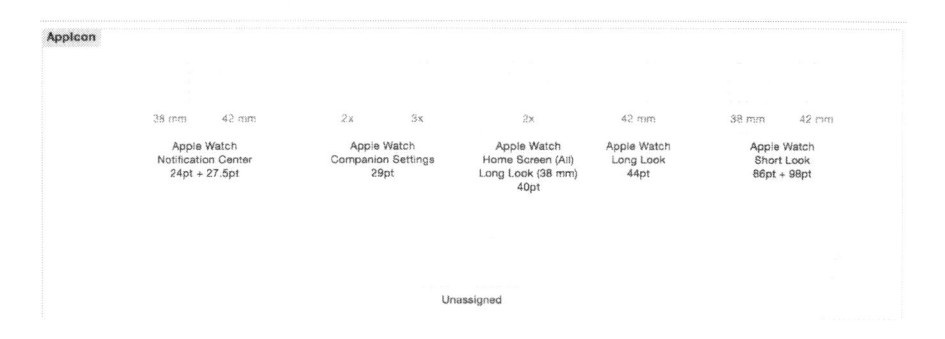

Figure 3.2 – The Xcode Asset file inside of a WatchKit app contains a spot to place each of the appropriately sized app icon files.

These icon files will be copied over to the watch when the user installs the app, ensuring they are always in the watch cache and ready for use.

The app icon for the watch app is what users will see most often. The following design tips will help making an eye catching and appropriate icon:

- **Keep it simple:** Consider how small the app icon will look when displayed on the watch screen. Add a single, simple element that captures the idea of the app.
- **Make it match:** A WatchKit app will have a companion iOS app; while the icons should be different, they should still have a similar look to assist the user in identifying them. Taking part of the iOS app icon to use for the WatchKit app icon will help users associate the WatchKit app with the iOS app.
- **Check it:** Watch icons on the 38mm and 42mm will be different sizes. Check the icon on each of these devices to ensure that the icon looks great at both sizes.
- **Use a designer:** Designers are skilled at ensuring visual consistency throughout an app's experience. When in doubt about how the app icon should look, allow a graphic designer to help with the design goals of the app.

Designing Image Assets

Icons aren't the only art that will be displayed on the Apple Watch. Almost any image can be displayed from a dynamic notification, or a WatchKit app through the use of an `WKInterfaceImage` object in the Storyboard (see Chapter 4, "Building watchOS User Interfaces with WatchKit Controls").

Custom images that are presented throughout an app can be any size, the following guidelines will help when designing custom images:

- Export PNG or PDF vector-based images and store them in XCAsset files in the Extension or App
- Don't use interlaced PNG files or PNG files with alpha channels
- Understand that black and darker images use less energy to display due to the way the screen functions,

- Use line weights that are appropriate for the type and complexity of glyph that will be displayed (Figure 3.3)

Type of Glyph	Apple Watch (38mm)	Apple Watch (42mm)
Complex line-based glyphs	5px	6px
Simpler line-based glyphs	8px	9px
Complex container shapes	4px	5px

Figure 3.3 – Line widths to use depending on the type and complexity of the custom glyph for custom graphics or for Force Touch menu images.

With WatchKit apps, each `WKInterfaceController` – the standard base UIView controller subclass inside of the app – can have additional options available to it through "Force Touch" menus. With this feature, it's possible to implement a menu system whereby up to 4 custom actions can be displayed overtop the view (Figure 3.4).

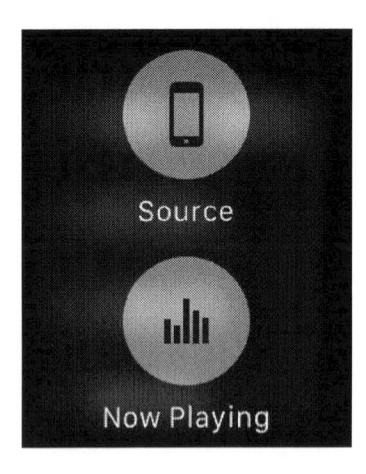

Figure 3.4 – A view of the Force Touch menu with icons in an Apple Watch app.

With Force Touch menu icons, only the glyph is created as a template image. watchOS will automatically format and display the image appropriately. Because they are template images, color information stored with the PNG is ignored. The alpha channel of the image defines the resulting shape when watchOS finishes processing it for display. Ensure that a border between the canvas size and the content of the icon is maintained so that the glyph displays properly inside of the icon.

Differences exist in the size of the menu icons depending on the screen size of the watch running the app. Because of this, follow the sizing guide in Figure 3.5 for formatting the glyphs that will display inside the menu icons.

Device	Canvas Size	Content Size
Apple Watch (38mm)	70 x 70	46 x 46
Apple Watch (42mm)	80 x 80	54 x 54

Figure 3.5 – The @2x pixel dimensions of the Force Touch menu icons for the 38mm and the 42mm Apple Watch.

Using the Image Cache

The image cache on Apple Watch allows for storing and retrieving frequently-used image files. The onboard image cache is limited to about 5MBs per app, and care should be taken to store only frequently-used files that would normally be costly to return to disk or iPhone to fetch.

The cache should be implemented in code. All of the caching methods below can be called on the `WKInterfaceDevice` singleton available by calling `[WKInterfaceDevice currentDevice]`.

Adding Cached Images

Cached images can either be added from an `UIImage` object or by passing in an `NSData` object containing image data.

To store a `UIImage`, use the following method call for each image object to be stored:

```
[[WKInterfaceDevice currentDevice]
addCachedImage:image name:@"key"];
```

Storing `NSData` representations of images follows the same approach:

```
[[WKInterfaceDevice currentDevice]
addCachedImageWithData:imageData name:@"key"];
```

Both methods return a `BOOL` value: `YES` when the image object was stored in the cache, and `NO` when the image object couldn't be stored in the cache.

Removing Cached Images

There are two ways to clear the image cache of images. The first is to remove a specific image using its name, which was originally set when the image was created:

```
[[WKInterfaceDevice currentDevice]
removeCachedImageWithName:@"key"];
```

This will immediately remove the image with the specified "key" `NSString` value from the device's image cache and will free the space for more images to be added later.
Clearing the entire cache so that all new images can be added into the cache is done with another method:

```
[[WKInterfaceDevice currentDevice]
removeAllCachedImages];
```

Once images are removed, the space is free and available for use again. Once the cache is filled, a `NO` is returned when attempting to cache images.

Getting Cached Image Size

The WatchKit app image cache is implemented as an `NSMutableDictionary`. To retrieve information for items store in the image cache, make a call to retrieve an object from the `NSDictionary` using the key specified while adding the image to the cache:

```
[[[WKInterfaceDevice currentDevice]
cachedImages]
objectForKey:@"key"];
```

An `NSNumber` object is returned that contains the size of the image stored for key in bytes so that it can smartly remove images from the cache, making room for other images.

Images stored in the watch app cache are loaded using `UIImage`'s standard `imageNamed:` method, and images stored in the cache will load much faster than their disk-stored counterparts.

Color

Color is an important topic when it comes to WatchKit. There are many ways to establish branding inside of WatchKit apps and notifications using color combinations that express the brand and design patterns.

Nearly any color can be used in interface elements such as labels, buttons, and other interface elements throughout WatchKit. This is accomplished through the color picker inside the Interface Builder Storyboards or in-code using the UIColor class programmatically.

There are certain areas in iOS, however, where caution should be taken about not only using color, but also about the colors are used:

- Ensure that apps use a black background. This is done to save power, as the screen is an AMOLED-based display, which uses less power to draw black colors than it does rendering bright colors. In addition to power-savings, the black background blends in with the Apple Watch bezel, giving the illusion of an edgeless screen design.
- To ensure legibility and contrast, always use light colors for text. This will make text much easier to read on the small screens of the watch.
- Be aware of accessibility technologies baked into the Apple Watch, such as the ability to turn on grayscale mode, options like these can change how the app is presented.
- When showing interactivity, color shouldn't be the only means to convey information. On the Apple Watch, buttons and lists have rectangular shaped buttons (called the "platter") to offer interactivity to the user (Figure 3.6). While you can change the color of labels on these buttons, you should never use a colored label by itself to add interactivity.

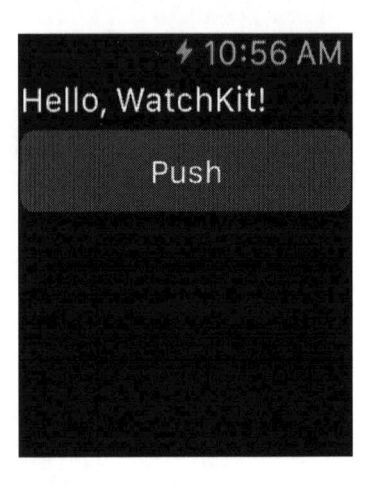

Figure 3.6 – The platter is used on tables, lists, and buttons to convey interactivity with those elements. This shows the user that the item is tappable.

Typography

Due to the relatively small screen size on the Apple Watch, font legibility is an important topic. In fact, this is such an important factor that Apple has designed a new font for the watch to improve legibility on the smaller screen.

The new font, called "San Francisco," is built into the WatchKit SDK. This new font works with the Dynamic Type system introduced with iOS 7, which automatically adjusts the font to fit the user's preference if using one of the built-in text styles.

San Francisco has two variants in the font styling, San Francisco Text and San Francisco Display (Figure 3.7). watchOS will automatically apply the most appropriate font depending on where the font is being used. For example, whenever there is a font being displayed below 19pt, the San Francisco Text is used; anything above 20pt uses the Display font variant.

San Francisco Text Regular

ABCDEFGHIJKLM

San Francisco Display Regular

ABCDEFGHIJKLM

Figure 3.7 – The two variants of the San Francisco font at various sizes.

Custom fonts can still be used on the watch, but there is no reason to use more than one custom font in each app. Apple notes in the HIG that using too many fonts in watch apps will make the interface feel disconnected from the rest of the system and other apps. Whenever using custom fonts, choose a larger font size to ensure legibility within the app.

Use the built-in font styles as much as possible. Doing so will ensure that the fonts will work with the Dynamic Text system on the watch and will conform to user preferences for font sizes throughout the watch and app interfaces.

Summary

In this chapter, you learned all about the design aspects surrounding Apple Watch apps, and a few of the key elements of the Human Interface Guidelines that Apple has provided to WatchKit app developers.

You've learned how to properly size icons for the app, and how the glyphs used for icons in force touch menus should be structured so they appear correctly on various sized Apple Watch screens. You've also learned how to work with the various XCAsset files to store your images in your app's bundle.

Finally, a key element of image storage on watchOS was covered: cached images. Through this image cache in WatchKit, you learned how to store images for very fast retrieval.

If you have further questions about any of the interface styles used through watchOS or WatchKit apps, you should consult the HIG (Apple Human Interface Guidelines). The new and updated HIG for Apple Watch can be found here:
https://developer.apple.com/watch/human-interface-guidelines.

Chapter 4: Advanced WatchKit Controls

Chapter Overview

WatchKit includes numerous user interface objects that can be used to build watchOS apps, which is critical since it's not possible to design custom `UIView` subclasses. One of the positives of WatchKit UI elements is that they don't require any knowledge or manipulation of Auto Layout constraints. Instead, objects automatically "flow" into place similar to `UICollectionView` elements in iOS, thus providing a consistent look and feel between all watchOS apps.

WatchOS shares many of the same UI elements as iOS, such as labels, switches, buttons, and more. In this chapter many advanced controls that can be used inside of WatchKit will be discussed in depth.

This chapter will demonstrate examples of how these objects work, as well as details on how to implement them inside of Interface Builder in your custom watchOS projects.

Group

Throughout the development of WatchKit user interfaces, the `WKInterfaceGroup` element will become an object that will be used frequently. They help guide interface layout decisions and provide an internal framework for managing on-screen controls with ease in a world without Auto Layout. However, this control does not have any visibility to the user and is akin to borderless

HTML tables that were typically used in early web development to layout elements on the screen.

`WKInterfaceGroup` objects are easy to implement: an object can be dragged into a Storyboard and configured with width, height, and position constraints from within the Attributes Inspector.

As an added benefit, groups can be configured with a background color, background image, corner radius, and content inset to provide an app with visual decoration not easily achieved using other interface elements in watchOS.

Figure 4.1 shows the types of interfaces that can be built using a group. It portrays a group with two nested subgroups. The main group (gray) has these properties:

- Width: Relative to Container
- Height: Relative to Container
- Layout: Horizontal

The left and right subgroup each have these properties:

- Width: Fixed, 67pt
- Height: Fixed, 100pt
- Horizontal: Left
- Vertical: Center

The left image (contained in left subgroup) and right image (contained in right subgroup) both have these identical properties:

- Width: Fixed, 50pt
- Height: Fixed, 50pt
- Horizontal: Center
- Vertical: Center

This type of nesting allows for a unique view hierarchy that you couldn't achieve without the use of groups.

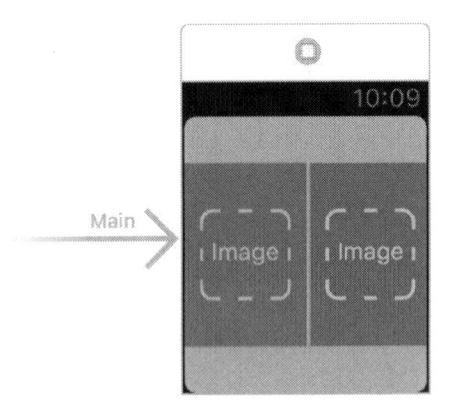

Figure 4.1 – WatchKit group with two nested subgroups, with each subgroup containing an image.

Table

iOS interfaces commonly use a `UITableView` implementation for displaying structured data. In WatchKit, tables are a great way to display data to user or provide navigation.

Tables in iOS and tables in WatchKit vary significantly: a table in watchOS has no cells, has no table or data source delegate methods that need to provide data to the table, nor does it have the Storyboard setup complexity required by iOS table view implementations. WatchKit tables have a single column similar to iOS, but can only have a single section.

Adding a table is done in the Storyboard file for the WatchKit app by dragging out a table object from the objects library onto the Storyboard scene (Figure 4.2). For the sample project, open the Top 10 app, then open the Interface.storyboard file from the Project Navigator, and locate the Main scene.

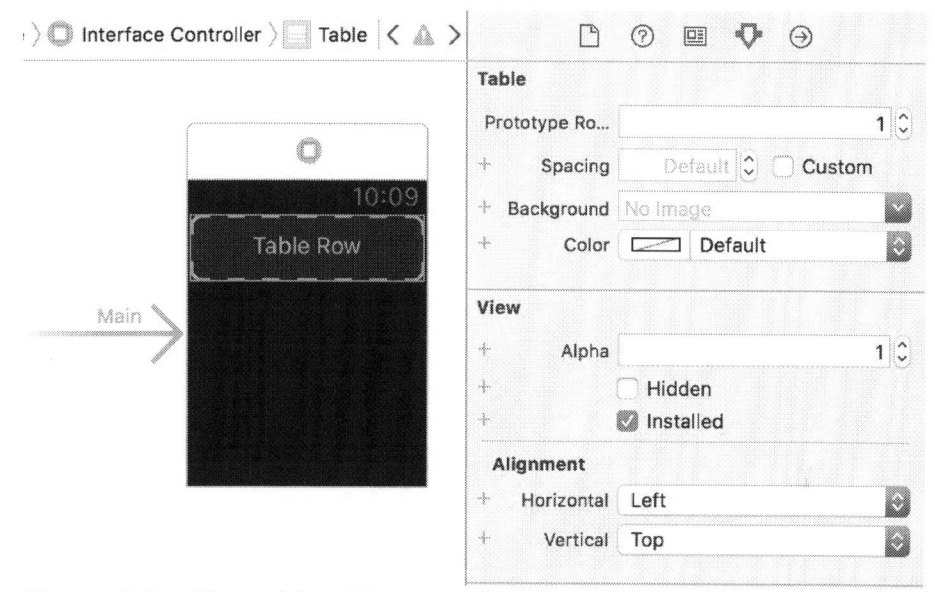

Figure 4.2 – The table object can be placed on any WKInterfaceController subclass and expands vertically as more Table Row types are added.

Selecting the table view in the Storyboard and opening the Attributes Inspector allows for additional settings. A few settings give the ability to add more than one prototype row, adjust the spacing, or set a background image or color on the table.

When adding a table view to the Storyboard, a Table Row Controller and an embedded group will also be created. The Table Row Controller is simply an `NSObject` that will be used to create `IBOutlets`, adding them to the interface elements in the embedded `WKInterfaceGroup`. This group can be resized and can contain multiple WatchKit UI elements such as labels and images placed inside to customize the look of the table row. Groups can also be nested to allow for more advanced layouts in the cell interface.

To customize the Top 10 app, add the following UI components to the table row:

Image

- Width: Fixed, 25pt
- Height: Fixed, 25pt
- Horizontal: Left
- Vertical: Center

Label

- Width: Relative to Container
- Height: Size to Fit Content
- Horizontal: Left
- Vertical: Center

The completed scene should look like Figure 4.3 below with the image and label added to the row controller.

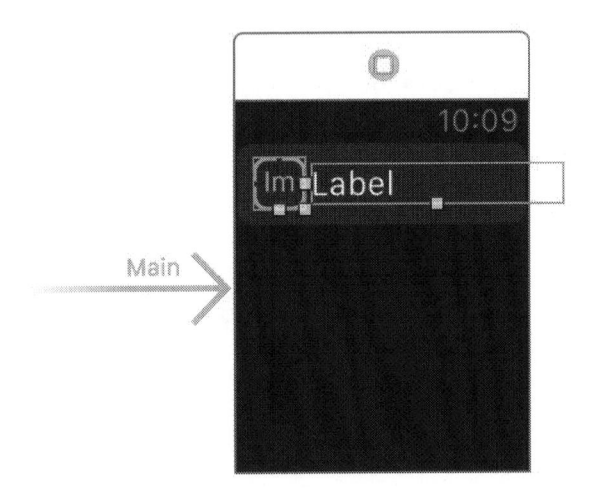

Figure 4.3 – The completed Table View Row for the Top 10 app main scene.

Now that a table row controller has been created in the Storyboard, an `NSObject` subclass named "MainRow" will need to be created for the code portion of the row controller, which will house `IBOutlet` references to the items contained in the Table Row Controller in the Storyboard. Edit the new MainRow header file to look like the code example that follows:

```objc
#import <Foundation/Foundation.h>
#import <WatchKit/WatchKit.h>
#import "JSONItem.h"

@interface MainRow : NSObject

@property (nonatomic, weak) IBOutlet WKInterfaceImage *image;

@property (nonatomic, weak) IBOutlet WKInterfaceLabel *label;

- (void)configureWithJSONItem:(JSONItem *)item
atIndex:(NSUInteger)index;

@end
```

Next, open MainRow.m and configure it to look like the following snippet of code. This code configures the method to lay out the row in the table view and can easily be called later in code, only passing in a JSONItem and the index for the row:

```objc
#import "MainRow.h"

@implementation MainRow

- (void)configureWithJSONItem:(JSONItem *)item
atIndex:(NSUInteger)index
{
    [self.image setImage:[UIImage
    imageNamed:@"MusicNote"]];
```

```
        [self.label setText:[NSString ⇥
        stringWithFormat:@"%u - %@", ⇥
            index + 1, item.songTitle]];
}

@end
```

After adding the code, return to the Storyboard containing the table. Select the Table Row Controller, then open the Identity Inspector and enter "MainRow" as the custom class for the row controller. Next, hook up the `IBOutlets` from the Main Row Controller to the image and label objects in the row controller group. Finally, with the Main Row Controller selected, open the Attributes Inspector and define an identifier for the row controller (use "MainRow").

To include multiple row controller types for different rows in the same table, repeat the steps above until the number of prototype rows desired has been created.

Now that the table row is configured, it is time to finish the implementation by adding code to control the table and provide the data to the table row objects for populating the table with data.

Open InterfaceController.m and add the following code:

```
#import "InterfaceController.h"
#import "NetworkController.h"
#import "JSONItem.h"
#import "MainRow.h"

@interface InterfaceController()

@property (nonatomic, weak) IBOutlet
WKInterfaceTable *table;
@property (nonatomic, strong) NSArray *jsonItems;

@end
```

```objc
@implementation InterfaceController

- (void)awakeWithContext:(id)context
{
    [super awakeWithContext:context];

    [[NetworkController sharedNetworkController] ➡
    retrieveJSONFeedWithCompletionHandler: ➡
    ^(NSError *error, NSArray *objects)
     {
        [self.table setNumberOfRows:objects.count ➡
           withRowType:@"MainRow"];

        for (NSUInteger row = 0; ➡
        row < self.table.numberOfRows; row++)
        {
            MainRow *currentRow = [self.table ➡
            rowControllerAtIndex:row];

            [currentRow configureWithJSONItem: ➡
            [objects objectAtIndex:row] ➡
            atIndex:row];
        }

        self.jsonItems = objects;
     }

    forNumberOfItems:10];
}
```

The preceding code is all that needs to be implemented in order for the table view to function. Before running the app, be sure to hook the table `IBOutlet` to the Main interface controller in the Storyboard so that InterfaceController.m has a reference to the table in the Storyboard scene.

Click Build and Run in Xcode with the WatchKit scheme selected, and the app will spring to life, and properly pull in the current top 10 songs available on the iTunes Store (Figure 4.4) and populate the table view.

Figure 4.4 – The completed main scene of the Top 10 sample app.

Picker

Pickers are used by many different apps in watchOS itself and are sometimes the single UI element included in an interface controller. Pickers in watchOS are similar to pickers in iOS except watchOS pickers also allow for easily selecting data on the smaller screen using the digital crown.

The watchOS picker consists of three varying implementations based on the type of data to be displayed: the list, sequence, and stack pickers (Figure 4.5), which are covered in this section.

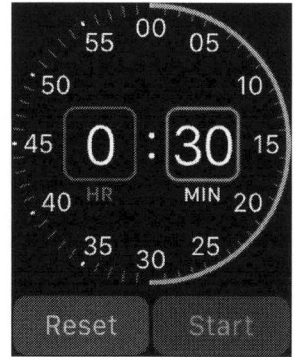

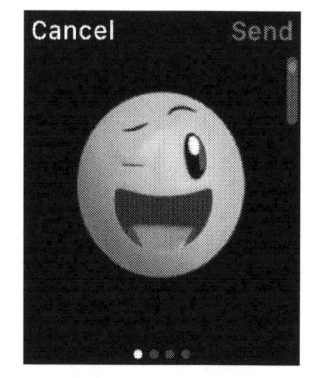

Figure 4.5 – The three types of WKInterfacePicker: from left to right: list, sequence, and stack.

List

The list picker type is an interface similar to the `UIPickerView` available on iOS. This picker type is designed for presenting the user with a list of data. This picker allows the developer to specify data that the user can scroll through with the Digital Crown in a 3D table style interface.

Sequence

By using the sequence style, the developer can create an interface tied to the rotation of the digital crown by the user. With this picker type through a delegate callback, the app can update multiple custom interface elements on the screen to achieve a desired UI effect, whether it's swapping out images, changing a label, or some other effect. An example of this type of picker is the built-in Timer app. As the user scrolls the Digital Crown, not only does the picker change the current number of minutes or seconds selected, but it also changes the background image used to represent the clock interface.

Stack

The stack picker is a vertically scrolling carousel type of view that is best used when several images need to be displayed. An example in watchOS is the animated emoji picker available throughout the system to find one of the included emojis.

Implementing a picker is done by first adding a picker object to the Interface Controller in the Storyboard from the Object Library (Figure 4.6). The Attributes Inspector can then be used to further customize the display of the picker.

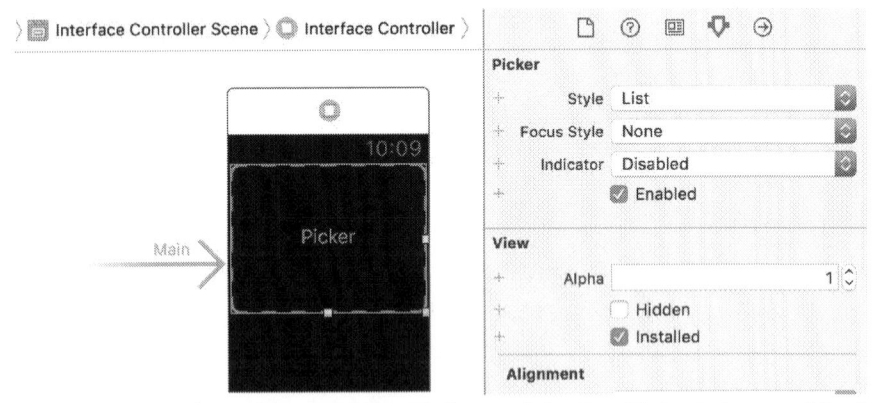

Figure 4.6 – The WKInterfacePicker with the List style enabled.

In the Attributes Inspector, there are three important properties that should be configured when implementing a picker interface: style, focus style, and indicator.

Style controls what picker type the scene will use: List, Stack, or Sequence are the possible choices for this property.

Focus Style refers to the outline around the picker when it is focused and ready to accept user input via the Digital Crown. By default, this is set to None but can also be set to Outline, which provides a green outline around the picker when focused. Additionally, Outline and Caption can be selected to provide a green outline around the picker when focused and use the caption string set on individual picker items to provide a caption area at the top of the picker.

Indicator refers to the small scroll indicator that is visible in the top right corner of the picker while scrolling with the Digital Crown. For an example of this behavior, look at the indicator in the animated emoji picker for watchOS. This indicator can either be disabled or shown while in focus. The indicator does not need to be shown if there is already sequential data displayed in the picker that gives the user a sense of context of the position in the list while scrolling. However, if users would not know where in the list they're currently positioned, as with the emoji picker, then displaying the indicator is recommended.

The following code sample shows implementing a List style picker with the default-selected attributes in Interface Builder.

Create an IBOutlet from the Storyboard to the picker property in code. Then in the `awakeWithContext:` method, add a code snippet that will populate the picker with data for the user to interact with, like this example that adds 10 items to the picker interface:

```
- (void)awakeWithContext:(id)context
  {
    [super awakeWithContext:context];

    NSMutableArray *itemsArray =
    [[NSMutableArray alloc] init];

    for (int i = 0; i < 10; i++)
    {
        WKPickerItem *item =
        [[WKPickerItem alloc] init];
```

```
        item.title = [NSString ➡
        stringWithFormat:@"Item %d", i];

        [itemsArray addObject:item];
    }

    [self.myAwesomePicker setItems:itemsArray];
}
```

This code example shows 10 `WKPickerItem` items, numbered sequentially, being added to an array called `itemsArray`. This is then set on the picker using the `setItems` method on the picker class, which will make the items visible to the user.

The `WKPickerItem` class has four properties that can be used when configuring the picker items: `ContentImage`, `Title`, `AccessoryImage`, and `Caption`.

ContentImage is useful when the main picker element the user will be selecting is made up of images. When the developer sets the the content image using a `WKImage` object, the image will be set on the picker interface when populated with the `WKPickerItems`.

Title is used whenever the main picker elements that the user will be selecting are strings. This property is only available to configure the List picker types.

AccessoryImage is an optional image that can be placed alongside the title string in the picker to add more clarity to the items that can be selected. The image should be a 13pt x 13pt image; larger images will be scaled down automatically by watchOS, but smaller images will just be centered and not scaled up automatically.

Caption only needs to be configured if the developer is using a Caption option in the picker style. Whenever the focus style of the picker is set to the Outline and Caption option, the picker will read this property on each of the `WKPickerItem` objects in order to set the caption field appropriately.

Once all the `WKPickerItems` have been added to the picker, the last step is to set the focus on the picker in order to allow user input. Do this by calling the `focus` method on the picker outlet.

The focus method will cause the picker to be responsive to user input via the Digital Crown. Rotating the crown will advance the picker, allowing the user to select a new value. At this stage, however, the picker wouldn't be of much value since the app isn't reading the new value.

In order for your code to get a callback whenever the picker value changes, assign the action of the picker in the Storyboard to an `IBAction` method with a signature like the following code sample:

```
- (IBAction)pickerValueChanged:(NSInteger)index
{
    //TODO: React to value change in the picker
}
```

Setting this method as the action for the picker in Interface Builder will cause this method to be called each time the user advances the picker by rotating the Digital Crown.

Map

Maps on such a small device pose many technical concerns, mainly affecting battery life. Fortunately, Apple has made significant progress balancing battery life against performance with the implementation of `WKInterfaceMap` on watchOS.

Whenever a `WKInterfaceMap` object is added to a watchOS interface and a location for display is specified, the map is generated as an image and displayed in the map interface object.

This reduces the need for dynamic map elements that could potentially pose battery life issues.

This tradeoff does mean that users cannot interact with the map; instead, tapping on the static map launches the Maps app on the and takes the user to the same location on an interactive display.

Even with these limitations, the map object still offers many features found on iOS. The following example code uses a set of 2D coordinates for Apple's 1 Infinite Loop headquarters to create a map and display an annotation on the map at that coordinate.

After a `WKInterfaceMap` object is added to a Storyboard scene, the rest of the map object is configured in code through an `IBOutlet` to the map object. The following code, which could be placed in the `awakeWithContext:` method in an interface controller, will set the location on the map using static coordinates:

```
@property (nonatomic, weak) IBOutlet WKInterfaceMap *map;

...

- (void)awakeWithContext:(id)context
  {
    [super awakeWithContext:context];

    CLLocation *infiniteLoop =
    [[CLLocation alloc]
    initWithLatitude:37.3321115
    longitude:-122.0307624];

    MKCoordinateSpan span =
    MKCoordinateSpanMake(0.1, 0.1);

    MKCoordinateRegion region =
    MKCoordinateRegionMake(
```

```
        infiniteLoop.coordinate, span);

        [self.map setRegion:region];

        [self.map ➡
        addAnnotation:infiniteLoop.coordinate ➡
        withPinColor:WKInterfaceMapPinColorGreen];
}
```

This code shows the similarities between the iOS map object and `WKInterfaceMap` found in watchOS – the majority of the same methods are available on watchOS for configuring maps, but the load and interactivity vary greatly from what's found on iOS.

Menus

Apple has touted Force Touch as one of the main features available to users on the watch. Whenever an app needs to implement additional options, a Force Touch menu can be used to accomplish this task. Chapter 3 ("Designing for Apple Watch") covers how to create icons for Force Touch menus and the design choices behind when those menus should be used in apps. This section will show how the menus are created in code and in the Storyboard file.

Menus can contain up to four menu items and, like the rest of the interface objects in watchOS, must be configured at design time in the Storyboard scene and cannot be configured dynamically at runtime. The menu is interface controller-specific – there can only be one menu per controller, but controllers can implement their own menu.

Add a menu to a Storyboard scene by dragging a Menu object out of the Object Library and onto the scene. This will add a menu object and an initial menu item to the scene. Up to three additional menu items can be added, as desired, to the interface controller scene. Select the Attributes Inspector for the Menu Item (Figure 4.7) to allow for customization of the menu item title and image.

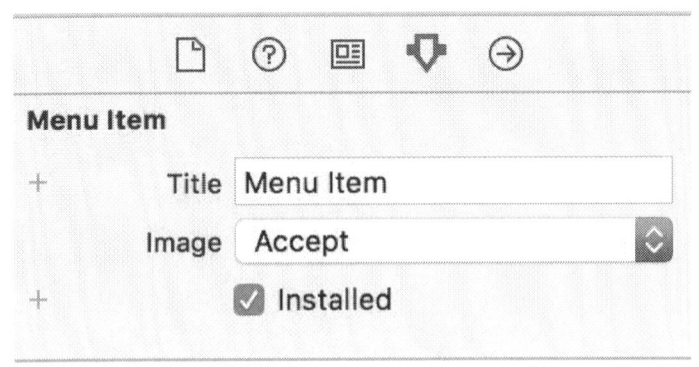

Figure 4.7 – The configuration options for a Menu Item in the Attributes Inspector.

By default, the image is set to Custom in the Attributes Inspector, which allows for a custom image to be picked from images from the `XCAssets` file. In addition, you can use any of Apple's template images in the list.

A standard `IBAction`, as in the following code snippet, is then used to intercept taps on the menu items to perform an action. Wire up the Action outlet from the Storyboard to the class to have the code called.

```
- (IBAction)menuItemTapped:(id)sender
{
    //TODO: React to menu item being tapped
}
```

It is important to note that if a Menu Item is implemented without an image assigned, the Menu Item will refuse to show when Force Touching the interface controller. When an app with a menu is run, Force Touch on the assigned interface controller to see the menu appear on screen (Figure 4.8).

Figure 4.8 – The menu being shown after a Force Touch on the interface controller.

Summary

Apple has put a great deal of care and design into creating the advanced WatchKit objects in this chapter. Because watchOS cannot accommodate custom interface controls, these objects will serve as the building blocks of all the watchOS apps you create throughout this publication and in your own app development.

In addition to learning about the basic and more advanced interface elements that are contained in this chapter, you set out to update the Top 10 app, implementing a table view that is capable of displaying the top song data from the iTunes Store feed.

In the chapters that follow, you'll continue building out the sample app. Along the way, you will learn more about how interface objects learned in this chapter serve as building blocks for all watchOS apps.

Going Further

In this chapter, you learned how to create an app menu that adds additional buttons to the user interface, buttons that are hidden until the user initiates a Force Touch on the containing interface controller.

The Top 10 sample app could use this functionality in order to refresh the table with the latest content. Tweak the sample project so that it has the following changes:

- Move the code to create the row controller to a separate method so that it can be called more than just when the interface controller awakens.
- Call the method above whenever the interface controller awakens so that it is populated with the content whenever the controller loads.
- Create a menu containing a single menu item called "Refresh" that calls the refresh method created above to refresh the interface with the newest content from the music store.

Remember that the sample code and completed going further code is available in both Objective-C and Swift from the book's companion website.

Chapter 5: WatchKit Multimedia

Chapter Overview

watchOS 2 introduced a number of multimedia components for developers to implement. From being able to play back small clips, to full audio playback support, to the ability to literally reach out and touch users with the Taptic Engine, there is a multimedia component for almost any type of app.

In this chapter the following multimedia features of watchOS will be covered in depth:

- Encoding used in watchOS for audio and video playback.
- Using the `WKInterfaceMovie` controller to play audio and video.
- Using `presentMediaPlayerControllerWithURL:` to programmatically load video.
- Recording audio with the built-in microphone.
- Using the haptic engine API to produce subtle taps and system sounds.

By the end of this chapter, you'll have learned all of the multimedia features in WatchKit and how to implement them.

Introduction to Video Playback in watchOS

Video playback is intended to allow users to play small snippets of content on their watches without having to open the companion app on their iPhone.

As is commonly said, "With great power comes great responsibility," and this is certainly true when dealing with video playback on an Apple Watch. You should only present users with small snippets of video: don't present anything longer than two minutes. While there is no technical limitation to video length on the watch, there are practical limitations involving battery life and the quality of the user experience. It should go without saying that no one wants to watch a feature-length movie on a watch.

Videos ported for the watch should follow standard encoding principles and should be formatted specifically for the device screen to minimize audio and video load times. The next section will cover how these multimedia files should be encoded to provide the best possible user experience.

Encoding

Video and audio on the Apple watch conform to the standard encoding practices that are also found on iOS, but in order to get the best audio and video quality while keeping a low file size, you need to understand Apple's intentions with encoding.

Apple has specified the recommended settings for the watch (Figure 5.1). These settings should be strongly enforced to maintain the best quality for the device while also minimizing the sizes of the files stored on the device or retrieved via the network.

Asset Type	Apple Recommended Encoding Settings
Video	Video codec: H.264 High Profile Video bit rate: 160 kpbs at up to 30 fps Full screen resolution: 208 x 260 portrait 16:9 resolution: 320 x 180 landscape Audio bit rate: 32 kpbs stereo
Audio	Bit rate: 32 kbps stereo

Figure 5.1 – Watch recommended multimedia encoding settings.

Once video and audio assets are properly encoded for the watch, the files can be easily transmitted over the network or loaded from disk, providing the best possible viewing experience for users on Apple Watch.

Playing Audio and Video with `WKInterfaceMovie`

With WatchKit, Apple introduced a new interface object called `WKInterfaceMovie` that enables easy drag and drop movie controls onto a Storyboard. Despite its name, `WKInterfaceMovie` supports both audio and video playback in a full screen mode and allows easy customization of an interface with multimedia elements.

Using the movie object is the quickest and easiest way to get multimedia content playing in WatchKit apps. To show how simple it is to use this new control, update the Top 10 app so that the sample code is retrieving the audio sample file.

Begin in the JSONItem.h file by adding the two new properties:

```
@property (nonatomic, strong) NSURL *imageURL;
@property (nonatomic, strong) NSURL ➡
*audioPreviewURL;
```

Navigate to the NetworkController.m file, and locate the method named `itemForDictionary:` and add the following lines before the return statement:

```
NSArray *imagePreviewArray = ➡
dictionary[@"im:image"];

item.imageURL = [NSURL ➡
URLWithString:[[imagePreviewArray ➡
lastObject] objectForKey:@"label"]];

NSArray *audioPreviewArray = dictionary[@"link"];

item.audioPreviewURL = [NSURL ➡
URLWithString:[[[audioPreviewArray ➡
lastObject] objectForKey:@"attributes"] ➡
objectForKey:@"href"]];

return item;
```

The code will further parse the JSON returned from the iTunes Store query, assigning the album art to be used for a movie poster to the `imageURL` property, and assigning the audio preview URL to the `audioPreviewURL` property.

With these two changes in place, the detail view for the Top 10 app can be completed. Open the Interface.storyboard, and create a new instance of the `WKInterfaceController`. Add a label, followed by a movie object, and stack them on top of each other so that they resemble Figure 5.2.

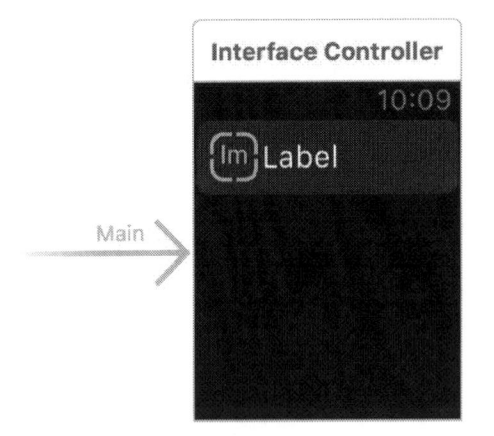

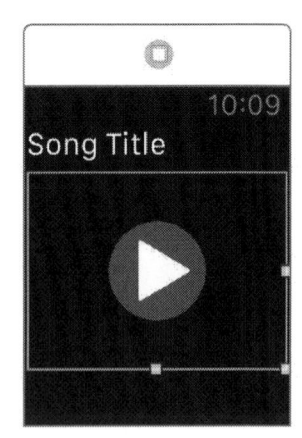

Figure 5.2 – The detail interface controller (right) that will be used to display the audio preview movie controller.

Next, click the Interface Controller and set the interface controller identifier of "detailController" on this detail view inside of the Attributes inspector. Then create a new `WKInterfaceController` subclass called "DetailController," and make the implementation file match the following code:

```
#import "DetailController.h"
#import "JSONItem.h"

@interface DetailController ()

@property (nonatomic, weak) IBOutlet ➡
WKInterfaceLabel *songTitleLabel;

@property (nonatomic, weak) IBOutlet ➡
WKInterfaceMovie *audioPreviewMovie;

@end

@implementation DetailController

- (void)awakeWithContext:(id)context
```

```objc
{
    [super awakeWithContext:context];

    JSONItem *detailItem = (JSONItem *)context;

    [self.songTitleLabel
    setText:detailItem.songTitle];

    [self.audioPreviewMovie
    setMovieURL:detailItem.audioPreviewURL];

    [self.audioPreviewMovie
    setPosterImage:[WKImage imageWithImageData:
    [NSData dataWithContentsOfURL:
    detailItem.imageURL]]];

    [self.audioPreviewMovie setLoops:NO];
}
@end
```

In the preceding code, outlets for both the label and the movie objects were added, which are configured in the `awakeWithContext:` method. Later a `JSONItem` object will be passed through this method as a context object, which will help configure the detail controller.

There are only 4 methods available on `WKInterfaceMovie`; two of them have already been implemented in the sample app.

Here's what each of these methods do:

`setMovieURL` method will accept an NSURL that represents the URL of the audio or video asset.

`setVideoGravity` method sets how the video will be resized in the control by passing in a `WKVideoGravity` enum. It should be noted that because the watch screen is mostly square, the video will be cropped by default.

`setPosterImage` method specifies a poster image that shows the content the user will be able to play when tapping the play button in the interface. This method exists because the movie control is inline with the content and specifying a static image that will appear with a play button on top of it provides a better user experience than just having a play button floating in the interface.

`setLoops` specifies whether or not the content will start over again at the beginning when it reaches the end. You can loop content by passing in `YES`; pass in `NO` otherwise. This value is set to `NO` by default.

The last addition to the detail controller is to ensure that the detail controller in the Storyboard is using the new `WKInterfaceController` subclass named DetailController, and that the `IBOutlets` are properly connected to their objects in the scene.

To tie everything together and make the detail view controller function properly, add a new table view delegate method to the main interface controller that will respond to the user tapping on a cell in the table view. To do this, open the InterfaceController.m file, and add the following method:

```objc
- (void)table:(WKInterfaceTable *)table
    didSelectRowAtIndex:(NSInteger)rowIndex
{
    JSONItem *jsonItem = [self.jsonItems
    objectAtIndex:rowIndex];

    [self pushControllerWithName:
    @"detailController" context:jsonItem];
}
```

This code pushes the `detailController` onto the navigation stack and passes in the `JSONItem` that needs to be populated as a context object.

Once the app has been built and is running, the movie poster image gets loaded in as soon as the detail interface finishes loading. Tapping on the Play button launches a movie player, which begins playing the song snippet (Figure 5.3).

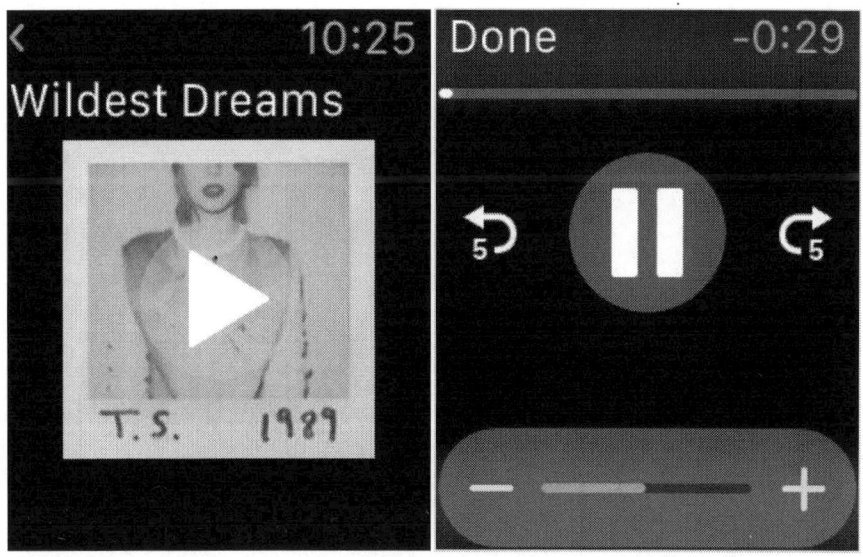

Figure 5.3 – The completed detail controller, which contains a movie player object for playing the audio preview.

Presenting the Media Controller Programmatically

The built-in `WKInterfaceMovie` object makes it is easy to get up and running quickly, but for more advanced implementations where an app may use a custom play button you should present the controller programmatically.

To use this presentation method, you'll simply need the media URL (either a local path on disk, or a network URL) and an `NSDictionary` of media player options and their keys, like this:

```
NSDictionary *options = @{
WKMediaPlayerControllerOptionsAutoplayKey:@YES,
WKMediaPlayerControllerOptionsStartTimeKey:@0,
WKMediaPlayerControllerOptionsVideoGravityKey:@0,
WKMediaPlayerControllerOptionsLoopsKey:@NO
};

[self presentMediaPlayerControllerWithURL: ➡
item.audioPreviewURL options:options ➡
completion:^(BOOL didPlayToEnd, NSTimeInterval ➡
endTime, NSError * _Nullable error) {

    //Called whenever the item finishes playing

}];
```

The `NSDictionary` passed in contains keys and values that relate to the properties that are set on the media object. There are also two new variables only available in the programmatically presented implementation: the ability to set the start time of the file playback, and the ability to set whether or not the item will begin auto playing when the media player is displayed.

When calling `presentMediaPlayerControllerWithURL:options:completion:`, pass in a completion handler block that will be invoked whenever the media player is dismissed either by the user or programmatically using the `[WKInterfaceController dismissMediaPlayerController]` method.

Unlike the media player object in the Storyboard, whenever the player is closed and the completion block is called, a `BOOL` value is passed in to determine if the user played the video to end. An

`NSTimeInterval` helps determine where the playhead time was at when the user closed the player. This completion block can be used for metrics tracking or reporting playback errors.

Recording Audio with Built-in Microphone

The Apple Watch includes a high-quality microphone that is used for phone calls, Siri, and text dictation. Starting in watchOS 2, third party apps can record audio using the built-in microphone, then store or transmit the recording over the network.

Starting a new recording is as easy as audio or video playback due to the convenient methods on `WKInterfaceController`. Before beginning, there are few basic pieces of information that should be covered. First, the audio recording UI is presented and controlled by watchOS, not by the third party app itself.

Next, there are presets used by the audio recorder to determine the quality of audio that can be captured. These presets are defined with the following `enum` values:

`WKAudioRecordingPresetNarrowBandSpeech` is used when doing a standard voice recording. This preset records audio with an 8 kHz sampling rate using either the LPCM 128 kbps or AAC 24 kbps format.

`WKAudioRecordingPresetWideBandSpeech` is used whenever higher-fidelity voice recordings are needed. This preset records audio with a 16 kHz sampling rate using either the LPCM 256 kbps or AAC 32 kbps format.

`WKAudioRecordingPresetHighQualityAudio` is used in high-quality audio recordings. This preset records audio with a 44.1 kHz sampling rate using either the LPCM 705.6 kbps or AAC 96 kbps format.

To start a recording, pass the audio recorder a local URL with the location where the completed recording will be stored. This URL will need to include an extension in order for the audio recorder to determine the type of audio file that is written to disk. Valid extensions in watchOS 2 are .wav, .mp4, or .m4a.

In order to configure audio recorder settings, pass the audio recorder an options `NSDictionary` object into the presentation method. This dictionary object can contain the following key value pairs to set the recorder options:

`WKAudioRecorderControllerOptionsActionTitleKey` This string determines the action button title in the alert player. The action button is the button in the recording interface that the user will tap to dismiss the recorder controller. An example to use here would be "Done," "Save," or some other action the user can take when they're finished recording.

`WKAudioRecorderControllerOptionsAlwaysShowActionTitleKey` When set to `YES`, the audio recorder will show the action button as soon as it's presented. When set to `NO`, the action button will only be presented if the user has recorded content.

`WKAudioRecorderControllerOptionsAutorecordKey` When set to `YES`, this value will cause the recorder controller to immediately start recording when presented. Setting NO will cause the recorder interface to appear, but not start recording automatically.

`WKAudioRecorderControllerOptionsMaximumDurationKey` This value sets the maximum length of the recorded clip. When this maximum length is reached, the audio recorder will stop recording.

To show the recording interface, call the `presentAudioRecorderControllerWithOutputURL:pr` eset:options:completion: method on the WKInterfaceController that will handle presentation.

The following sample code shows the code required to present an audio recorder, complete with the path to store the file in the app's documents directory:

```
NSArray *filePaths = NSSearchPathForDirectoriesInDomains( NSDocumentDirectory, NSUserDomainMask, YES);

NSString *path = [[filePaths firstObject] stringByAppendingPathComponent:@"recording.mp4"];

NSURL *fileURL = [NSURL fileURLWithPath:path];

[self presentAudioRecorderControllerWithOutputURL: fileURL preset: WKAudioRecorderPresetHighQualityAudio options:nil completion:^(BOOL didSave, NSError * _Nullable error)
{
    //Handle recording file here
}];
```

When this method is called, pass in the file URL discussed previously, the desired audio preset, the options dictionary (specify a nil dictionary if you want to use the default values), and a completion handler. The completion handler block has BOOL and NSError values that will be returned when the recording controller is exited by tapping the action button in the controller.

It is important to note that passing in a file URL that is outside of the app sandbox will result in the presentation of the audio controller, but doing so will generate an error after the user closes the recording interface.

Audio Playback

`WKInterfaceMovie` allows your apps to play back media files easily inside of the app, but, what if a custom interface for audio-only multimedia playback is required? watchOS can handle this use case, and will even allow apps to continue playing audio while backgrounded.

To implement a custom solution and interface, you can use a new class introduced in watchOS 2 called `WKAudioFilePlayer` (or `WKAudioFileQueuePlayer` for setting up a playlist of multiple audio items). This class can be used for audio-only files.

The following sample code demonstrates how to create a queue player programmatically with three player items. To begin, instantiate a `WKAudioFileAsset` object for each of the audio files you wish to play in the player:

```
WKAudioFileAsset *file1 = [WKAudioFileAsset
assetWithURL:file1URL ➡
title:@"Danger Zone" albumTitle:@"Self" ➡
artist:@"Cory"];

WKAudioFileAsset *file2 = [WKAudioFileAsset ➡
assetWithURL:file2URL ➡
title:@"Screendoor" albumTitle:@"Self" ➡
artist:@"Kyle"];

WKAudioFileAsset *file3 = [WKAudioFileAsset ➡
assetWithURL:file3URL ➡
title:@"On a Boat" albumTitle:@"Self" ➡
artist:@"Beau"];
```

When instantiating the `WKAudioFileAsset`, optionally specify metadata like the title of the audio file, the album title, and the artist. If the audio files do not have this associated metadata simply use the `assetWithURL:` method instead. Whether or not the metadata is present, the user will be able to play, pause, and skip tracks in watchOS.

The `WKAudioFilePlayer` class does not handle `WKAudioFileAsset`s directly, so these assets must be wrapped inside of another object called `WKAudioFilePlayerItem`.

```
WKAudioFilePlayerItem *file1Item =
[WKAudioFilePlayerItem
playerItemWithAsset:file1];

WKAudioFilePlayerItem *file2Item =
[WKAudioFilePlayerItem
playerItemWithAsset:file2];

WKAudioFilePlayerItem *file3Item =
[WKAudioFilePlayerItem
playerItemWithAsset:file3];
```

This code calls the `playerItemWithAsset:` method and passes in the `WKAudioFileAsset` in order to create the instance of `WKAudioFilePlayerItem`. This object manages the state of the asset being played and lets apps easily observe the state of the asset by checking the `status` property on the objects.

The status returns one of the following enums:

`WKAudioFilePlayerItemStatusUnknown` is returned when the status of the player item is unknown. Check the status property again later to see if the status has updated.

`WKAudioFilePlayerItemStatusReadyToPlay` is returned whenever the file has been loaded, verified, and can now be passed into the player for playing.

`WKAudioFilePlayerItemStatusFailed` is returned whenever there was an error that occurred while loading the file and the file cannot be played by the audio player.

A single instance of `WKAudioFileAsset` can be passed to the `WKAudioFilePlayer`, but this example uses multiple items that will be passed to the player. `WKAudioFileQueuePlayer` is required since it can handle an array of multiple items and create a playlist for the player.

To instantiate a new `WKAudioFileQueuePlayer`:

```
self.audioPlayer = [WKAudioFileQueuePlayer queuePlayerWithItems:@[file1Item, file2Item, file3Item]];
```

To be able to configure and control the player programmatically, store the audio player as a property on the class. The audio player class has several methods that, coupled with interface elements, can let users control the playback of the audio items:

`play` can be called whenever the current item should be played.

`pause` can be called when the player should be pause playback.

`currentItem` can be called to get the current `WKAudioFilePlayerItem` object.

`currentTime` can be called to get the current play head position (which is also the play time elapsed) in an `NSTimeInterval` format.

The `items` object is an array of `WKAudioFilePlayerItem` objects that are currently set on the player. The following four methods are available exclusively to queue players:

`advanceToNextItem` is available on a queue player, stops playing the current item, and then loads and begins playing the next item in the queue.

`appendItem:` is available on the queue player, adds another item to the end of the queue by passing in a new `WKAudioFilePlayerItem` object.

`removeItem:` is available on the queue player, removes an item currently in the queue by passing the item to be removed.

`removeAllItems` is available on the queue player, removes all the items in the current player queue so they are not played next.

Once the `play` method is called on the queue player, the player will begin playing the first item in the queue and will continue to play additional items sequentially until it reaches the end of the array.

Haptic Feedback and Sounds

One of the biggest advancements in terms of user interaction on the Apple Watch is the introduction of haptic feedback, which allows the software to tap the user on the wrist, providing a gentle nudge to confirm some action or to communicate basic information. Implementing haptic feedback is possibly the easiest one line of code that will have the greatest impact on the user interface design.

There are several built-in haptic feedback types defined by the `WKHapticType` enum. Below is the full list of the haptic feedback types that ship with watchOS:

`WKHapticTypeNotification` is the same alert and haptic feedback that the user receives from a local or push notification on their watch.

`WKHapticTypeDirectionUp` indicates that a user has provided input beyond a certain threshold, such as scrolling too far up on a table view with the Digital Crown.

`WKHapticTypeDirectionDown` indicates that a user has provided input below a certain threshold, such as scrolling too far down on a table view with the Digital Crown.

`WKHapticTypeSuccess` indicates the successful completion of a task.

`WKHapticTypeFailure` indicates the failed completion of a task.

`WKHapticTypeRetry` indicates that the user is retrying a task that may have previously failed.

`WKHapticTypeStart` indicates the beginning of an action.

`WKHapticTypeStop` indicates the completion of an action.

`WKHapticTypeClick` indicates the simplest click type of feedback. This can be used to mark specific fixed paths during a flow.

Use these `enums` by passing them to the method `playHaptic:` on `WKInterfaceDevice`:

```
[[WKInterfaceDevice currentDevice] ➡
playHaptic:WKHapticTypeStart];
```

As soon as this method is called, the haptic sound and associated vibration feedback is played for the user.

Summary

In this chapter you learned all about the multimedia components in watchOS and how to implement them in your own apps. In addition, you added a multimedia component to the Top 10 sample app, allowing audio playback.

Using multimedia components, users can easily view items that were previously relegated to iOS apps only right on their wrists, adding more immersion for apps that rely on multimedia components. Lastly, this chapter covered using the audio recorder to add recording functionality, and using haptics in apps to make user taps more responsive and overall provide a more responsive experience for the user.

Going Further

In this chapter, you updated the Top 10 app so that when the user taps on a main table row, they are immediately brought into the detail view to preview the song title they tapped. You also learned how to implement haptic feedback inside of the user interface. Use this Going Further opportunity to update the InterfaceController interface so that whenever the user taps on a table row, the haptic feedback `WKHapticTypeClick` is played.

Chapter 6: The Watch Connectivity Framework

Chapter Overview

In the initial version of WatchKit, Apple used `openParentApplication:reply:` to share data between the parent app and the WatchKit app. However, this method often fell short of what developers needed and so has been deprecated and is completely unavailable starting in watchOS 2.0.

With the second version of WatchKit, the Watch Connectivity Framework is provided to give developers a powerful, robust set of tools to handle almost any data transfer scenario. Through this set of tools, various content transfers and updates are handled seamlessly by watchOS. This framework manages bi-directional transfers between apps with ease.

This chapter will cover working with the Watch Connectivity Framework in order to send data to and receive data from the parent iOS app; the following subjects will be explained in depth:

- Setting up and managing `WCSession` connections
- Using the two types of communication categories appropriately
- Using background transfers for app context, user info, and files
- Using interactive message transfers for live communication and triggering events in iOS or watchOS

This chapter will also cover updating the Top 10 sample app to use Watch Connectivity for sharing data from the watch app to the iOS app.

Setting up a `WCSession` connection

`WCSession` is the class that is used to create a transfer session between a watchOS device and an iOS device. The sole purpose of this class is to facilitate the various transfer methods.

The class in the app handling the `WCSession` setup and callbacks, such as the `WKExtensionDelegate`, should be available when the app launches from the background and not set up inside of a `WKInterfaceController` subclass. The setup should also be performed as soon as possible during the app lifecycle.

The Top 10 app will be updated throughout this chapter to sync the downloaded album artwork from the watch or iOS app so the cached artwork is available on all devices, without additional, unnecessary network requests.

Create a new class called `SessionManager` that is available to both the iOS and WatchKit Extension targets. Once this `NSObject` subclass has been created, implement the following code to facilitate the singleton setup handling and the creation of the `WCSession`.

In the `SessionManager` header file:

```
#import <Foundation/Foundation.h>

@interface SessionManager : NSObject

+ (instancetype)sharedManager;

@end
```

Modify the SessionManager.m implementation file with the following code:

```objc
#import "SessionManager.h"
@import WatchConnectivity;

@interface SessionManager () <WCSessionDelegate>

@property (nonatomic, strong) WCSession *session;

@end

@implementation SessionManager

+ (instancetype)sharedManager {
    static SessionManager *sharedManager = nil;
    static dispatch_once_t onceToken;
    dispatch_once(&onceToken, ^{
        sharedManager = [[self alloc] init];
        [sharedManager configureSession];
    });
    return sharedManager;
}

- (void)configureSession
{
    if (![WCSession isSupported]) {
        return;
    }
    
    self.session = [WCSession defaultSession];
    self.session.delegate = self;
    [self.session activateSession];
}

@end
```

Before instantiating any session code, check to ensure the `isSupported` property on `WCSession` returns `YES`. When true it means that the device is compatible with the WC framework and a session can be created.

Next, request the `defaultSession`, then set the delegate to the session manager, and finally call `activateSession` to let the `WCSession` object know the app is ready to accept messages.

Understanding the Session State

In the previous section you used the state property available on `WCSession` called `isSupported`. This property allows the app to determine if it will continue setting up the `WCSession` based on whether or not the app is running on a compatible device (Apple Watch or iPhone — note that other iOS devices are not supported because they cannot pair with the watch).

To determine whether or not the watch app is installed on the watch, query the `watchAppInstalled` property on `WCSession`.

If the app is ready to send data, the `reachable` property should be checked on `WCSession`. This property behaves differently when queried on an iPhone than when it is queried on the Apple Watch. What follows is an explanation of the differences.

iPhone: When `reachable` is queried on the iPhone, a `YES` returned value will indicate that the watch is connected to the iPhone either by Bluetooth or Wi-Fi, and that the WatchKit app is running foreground on the watch; otherwise, a value of `NO` will be returned.

Apple Watch: When `reachable` is queried on the Apple Watch, a `YES` returned value will indicate that the iPhone is connected to the Apple Watch either by Bluetooth or Wi-Fi; otherwise, a value of `NO` will be returned.

Lastly, you can check the status of whether or not the users of the app have a companion watch face complication (covered in Chapter 7: "Building complications with ClockKit") enabled through the property named `complicationEnabled` on `WCSession`. Check this complication if complication-specific data is being shared from the iOS or watchOS app.

WCSession Delegate Methods

The WC Framework uses delegate methods introduced in watchOS 2.2 to ensure that both the sending and receiving app can be notified of errors that might occur during the transfer process.

There are three required methods from the `WCSessionDelegate`, two on iOS and one on watchOS. Below is an explanation of how each method is used.

On watchOS, the only required `WCSessionDelegate` is the delegate method `session:activationCompleteWithState:error:`. This method will be called whenever a `WCSession` object has been activated, and will provide the current state as a `WCSessionActivationState` constant, and an error if a connection issue occurred.

On iOS, two methods from the `WCSessionDelegate` need to be implemented. The first is `sessionDidBecomeActive:` which is called whenever a `WCSession` object has been activated, and passes in that active object as a parameter. The second method is `sessionDidDeactivate:`, which is called when a `WCSession` object goes from active state to an inactive state. For context in this method, the inactive `WCSession` object is passed as a parameter.

This required watchOS method needs to be implemented in the `SessionManager` class before it can be used to send and receive data. This method will be used to print errors to the console by including an `NSLog` statement inside of the delegate method in `SessionManager.m`:

```objc
- (void)session:(WCSession *)session
activationDidCompleteWithState:
(WCSessionActivationState)activationState
error:(NSError *)error {
    if (error) {
        NSLog(@"Unable to activate WCSession:
        %@", error.localizedDescription);
    }
}
```

Watch Connectivity Framework Communication Categories

There are many uses for the WC Framework and for each of these there is a category and matching methods that can accommodate the transfer of data between the watch app and the parent iOS app.

There are two primary types of transfer categories: background transfers and interactive messaging. The following sections take an in-depth look at both of these categories.

Background Transfers

Background transfers are the preferred approach whenever there is data that can be lazily transferred to the iOS or watchOS app. With this method, the operating system will intelligently select the most reasonable time to make the transfer so that whenever the iOS or watchOS app next launches, it will have the data available. A background transfer should be used when data isn't needed immediately.

Interactive Messaging

Interactive Messaging is the best approach if a watchOS apps requires the immediate transfer of data between the parent and watch app. This method permits live communication between the apps, and the ability to instantly transfer data over that live connection. Interactive Messaging can also be used for triggering specific events in the parent app.

In the following section both transfer methods will be discussed at a code level.

Implementing Background Transfers

Background transfers are recommended by Apple to let the operating system perform the data movement request lazily and at the most opportune time. With this lazy request, the app will be notified whenever new data is available during launch.

There are three types of background transfers, each of which is discussed later in this section:
- App context transfers, which send a very simple set of content updates via `WCSession`,
- User info transfers, which send a user info dictionary, and
- File transfers that queue up items such as image files.

With background transfers, whenever context, user info dictionary, or a file to be transferred is specified, it will not transfer immediately. Instead, the sending app stores the data in a temporary location, and when the sending device has an opportunity, the data will be transferred to a temporary location on the receiving device. Whenever the receiving app launches, the data will be passed into the app through delegate callbacks.

Background Transfer: App Context

App Context is an `NSDictionary` that gets transferred in the background and contains the most up-to-date, important piece(s) of data the receiving app needs the next time it launches.

An example of how this might be used is if there is an iOS app where a user has logged into an account; any tokens or account credentials the Apple Watch might need can be packaged up into an `NSDictionary` and sent to the watch using Background App Context transfers. Whenever the watch app is launched, the `NSDictionary` will have the pertinent information needed to authenticate the user.

The `NSDictionary` can contain any standard property list types. The app context is considered the most up-to-date data, because whenever a new app context is transferred, the existing queued app context is replaced with the newest version, and is then transferred over to the receiving side lazily.

Configuring the Sender for Background App Context Transfer

In order to configure the app context, you will use a property on the `WCSession` singleton called `applicationContext`. This property stores the most up-to-date context from the sending side. In order to make a change to this property and add a new app context to be sent to the receiving side, call the `updateApplicationContext:error:` method on the `WCSession` singleton, passing in the `NSDictionary` containing the new app context and a pass by reference `NSError` object to check for any errors.

Whenever this process is completed successfully, the `applicationContext` property will be updated with the new set of data, and the OS will transfer the data to the receiver whenever it has a chance. If an error is returned, it will most likely be due to attempting to store non-property list data types in the `NSDictionary`.

See Figure 6.1 for the full list of valid property list data types.

Abstract Type	XML Element	Cocoa Class	Core Foundation Type
Array	`<array>`	NSArray	CFArray
Dictionary	`<dict>`	NSDictionary	CFDictionary
String	`<string>`	NSString	CFString
Data	`<data>`	NSData	CFData
Number - Integer	`<integer>`	NSNumber (`intValue`)	CFNumber
Number Floating Point	`<real>`	NSNumber (`floatValue`)	CFNumber
Boolean	`<true />` or `<false />`	NSNumber (`boolValue`)	CFBooleanRef; kCFBooleanTrue; kCFBooleanFalse

Figure 6.1 – The valid property list types for use in app context

The following code example shows the background app context transfer initiation on the sending side:

```
NSDictionary *newValue = @{@"myNewValue" : @"1"};

__autoreleasing NSError *error;

[[WCSession defaultSession]
updateApplicationContext:newValue
error:&error];
```

Check the output BOOL value to see if an error occurred, for more information on the error, check the `NSError` object; if the call succeeded, then the `NSDictionary` transfer has been queued and will be transferred to the receiving app.

Configuring the Receiver for Background App Context Transfer

Now that sending has been completed, it's up to the receiving side to check and retrieve the data from the `WCSession` singleton.

There are two ways that the receiving app can get the new app context dictionary. The first is by manually checking the property `receivedApplicationContext` on the `WCSession` singleton. This property contains the most recent `NSDictionary` object received from the sender.

Another approach is by using a delegate callback. To use this method, add the following delegate method to the class registering itself as a `WCSession` delegate:

```
- (void)session:(WCSession *)session ➡
didReceiveApplicationContext: ➡
(NSDictionary<NSString *,id> *)applicationContext
{
    //TODO: Handle new context data here
}
```

Whenever this method gets called, the new application context dictionary will be passed in, allowing the app to parse it. If a newer app context is transferred while the app is running, then this method will be called again.

These are all the steps necessary to take full advantage of app context background transfers between watchOS and iOS apps.

Background Transfer: User Info Dictionary

Similar to App Context transfers, User Info Dictionary transfers use an `NSDictionary` that gets passed from the sending side to the receiving side. Unlike App Context transfers, however, this method allows multiple dictionaries to be queued, and the queue holds onto the currently pending transfers until the OS is ready.

Configuring the Sender for Background User Info Dictionary Transfers

The following code example shows how to set up the transfer of a user info dictionary in the sending app:

```
NSDictionary *newValue = @{@"currentLevel" : @"1"};

WCSessionUserInfoTransfer *transfer = [[WCSession defaultSession] transferUserInfo:newValue];
```

This code packages up a value inside of an `NSDictionary` object, then calls `transferUserInfo:` on the `WCSession` singleton, passing in the dictionary object to the receiving app.

After the transfer the Watch Connectivity Framework will return a `WCSessionUserInfoTransfer` object, allowing the app to capture the object for performing additional operations. The `transferring` property holds a `BOOL` determining whether or not the data is still being transferred. In addition, you can use the `cancel` method on the transfer object if the app needs to cancel a transfer. Calling the cancel method will remove the object from the transfer queue if the data has not yet been sent; if it's already been sent, then calling this method has no effect.

There is also a way to look at all of the current outstanding transfers and optionally iterate over them and cancel or check the status of the transfers. To do this, use the `outstandingUserInfoTransfers` property on the `WCSession` singleton, which is an `NSArray` containing pending `WCSessionUserInfoTransfer` objects.

When the transfer is complete, the delegate on the receiving side will receive a callback to `session:didFinishUserInfoTransfer:error:`. This method will be called for each of the transfers in the queue.

Configuring the Receiver for Background User Info Dictionary Transfers

Whenever the app receives new data from the sender, the registered `WCSession` delegate class will get a callback to the delegate method `session:didReceiveUserInfo:`. This method will have the transferred `NSDictionary` passed in.

```
- (void)session:(WCSession *)session 
didReceiveUserInfo:(NSDictionary<NSString *,id> 
*)userInfo
{
    //TODO: Parse the transferred dictionary here
}
```

The method is called and run on a non-main queue, which will require switching to the main queue using `dispatch_async` if the app needs to update any UI elements from this delegate callback.

Background Transfer: File

If there are files that need to be the File transfer background method that can be used. With this method, nearly any file type can be transferred. One example would be an iOS app that shows photos and lets the user save to their favorites for on-the-go viewing on the watch. A background File transfer can sync those favorites to the watch for viewing the next time the user opened the watch app.

Similar to User Info Dictionary transfers, the background File transfer also uses a queue, a property on `WCSession` called `outstandingFileTransfers`. This queue contains `WCSessionFileTransfer` objects that also have a transferring property and a cancel method.

When a file is transferred, the delegate method `session:didReceiveFile:` will be called on the receiving side. Passing in the `WCSessionFile` object indicates the file URL where it will be located. Transferred files reside in the receiving app's /Documents/Inbox folder and can be moved out of that location into a more appropriate location using standard `NSFileManager` methods.

While this API allows for the transfer of large files, it's important to note that using this method can take a longer time to transfer, depending on file size. This is due to power constraints on the watch, and the OS waiting for the most opportune time to make the transfer happen.

Configuring the Sender for Background File Transfers

Configuring the sender begins with determining the URL for the file that will be transferred. This URL can be for any file stored in the application's container. The second item that may optionally be transferred is associated metadata.

Transferred metadata is stored as an `NSDictionary` representation. Apple recommends keeping this metadata dictionary as small as possible. The metadata will be transferred along with the file and will be available at the same time on the receiving side.

```
NSURL *fileURL = self.fileURL;
NSDictionary *metadata = @{@"myIdentifier" : ➡
@"1"};

[[WCSession defaultSession] transferFile:fileURL➡
metadata:metadata];
```

To begin the file transfer from the sending side, call the `transferFile:metadata:` method on the `WCSession` object. Similar to background User Info Dictionary transfers, calling this method will return a `WCSessionFileTransfer` object that contains properties for the file URL being transferred as well as the metadata dictionary. The app can also iterate over the files that are awaiting transfer by checking the `outstandingFileTransfers` property on the `WCSession` singleton, which will return an `NSArray` of `WCSessionFileTranfer` objects.

Configuring the Receiver for Background File Transfers

When the receiving app gets a new file transferred, it will have its `WCSession` delegate `session:didReceiveFile:` called, and the `WCSessionFile` object — the object that contains a `fileURL` property and the `metadata` as an `NSDictionary` — passed into this method.

It is important to note that the file being transferred is not automatically moved into the app's documents container and the file being transferred will need to be manually moved into a permanent location. Be sure to handle this move within the method, since the file will be removed from the temporary location once the delegate method returns.

This code sample shows configuring the receiver to accept a new file transfer:

```objc
- (void)session:(WCSession *)session
didReceiveFile:(nonnull WCSessionFile *)file
{
    NSURL *fileToMoveURL = file.fileURL;

    NSArray *filePaths =
    NSSearchPathForDirectoriesInDomains
    (NSDocumentDirectory, NSUserDomainMask,YES);

    NSString *path = [[filePaths firstObject]
    stringByAppendingPathComponent:
    [fileToMoveURL lastPathComponent]];

    NSURL *newLocationURL = [NSURL
    fileURLWithPath:path];

    NSError *error = nil;

    [[NSFileManager defaultManager]
    moveItemAtURL:fileToMoveURL toURL:
    newLocationURL error:&error];

    if (error)
    {
        NSLog(@"Error moving file: %@",
        error.localizedDescription);
    }
}
```

`NSFileManager` is used to move the file from the temporary path inside of the Documents/Inbox into the Documents directory.

Implementing Interactive Messaging

When an iOS or watchOS app needs to have live communication with its companion app, then interactive messaging can be implemented using the Watch Connectivity Framework. Data can be immediately transferred in real time using this approach.

An example of using interactive messaging between paired watchOS and iOS apps would be in an iOS game whereby an auxiliary display is used on the Apple Watch to select special items in the game. This type of feature would need to be low-latency and near instant.

In order to use interactive messaging, a few requirements first need to be met:

1. The iPhone and Apple Watch must be paired
2. The Apple Watch must be tethered via Bluetooth or Wi-Fi with the iPhone
3. The apps must both be reachable, which can be checked using the `reachable` property on the `WCSession` object.

The concept of reachable is different depending on the app. For the watch to be reachable from the iPhone, both devices must be connected, and the watchOS app must be in the foreground. For the iOS app to be reachable from the watch, both devices must be connected and the WatchKit extension must be in the foreground, not using a Complication.

When all of these conditions are met, then the `BOOL reachable` property on `WCSession` will be true, indicating the ability to use interactive messaging between the two apps.

When using interactive messaging from Apple Watch to iPhone, the iPhone app does not need to be in the foreground. This is because the iOS app can be launched from the background in order to perform a task or respond to incoming messages.

There are two types of interactive messaging: One that uses an `NSDictionary` to transmit the data using property list types, and one that uses `NSData` to send a string of data between the apps. The latter method is useful if the app has its own serialization format or custom data format that is best handled by the app without an `NSDictionary` intermediary.

Interactive Messaging with a Dictionary

Using the dictionary method of interactive messaging is very similar to the other methods of background data transfer, except the transfer will happen live and will be processed immediately.

Configuring the Sender for Interactive Messaging with a Dictionary

The following code example shows setting up the sending side of an interactive messaging session using an `NSDictionary` as the intermediary for the data:

```objc
if ([[WCSession defaultSession] reachable]) {
    NSDictionary *transferDict = @{@"myData": 
    @"1"};

    [[WCSession defaultSession] 
    sendMessage:transferDict 
    replyHandler:^(NSDictionary<NSString *,id>* 
    _Nonnull replyMessage)
    {
        if (replyMessage)
        {
            //TODO: Handle reply here
        }
    } errorHandler:^(NSError * _Nonnull error) {
        if (error)
```

```
        {
            //TODO: Handle error here
        }
    }];
}
```

In this code example, the first step is to check the `reachable` property to ensure the recipient device is reachable. Next, the data to be transferred is packaged in an `NSDictionary` object. Finally, the `sendMessage:replyHandler:errorHandler:` method is called on the `WCSession` object. The reply handler is an optional parameter, and if the recipient app will not respond on the sending side after the request has been transferred, then `nil` can be substituted for the block parameter. It is recommended that a reply handler is implemented, if only to ensure duplicate requests are not attempted.

Lastly, the `errorHandler` is required and should always be implemented to handle any errors the app receives during the transfer process. This error block will be called whenever the message was not successfully delivered.

Configuring the Receiver for Interactive Messaging with a Dictionary

When the receiving app receives an interactive message with an `NSDictionary`, one of two methods will be called, depending on whether the sending app supplied a reply handler or not. Since the method shown in the preceding sample code included a reply handler, the `WCSessionDelegate` callback is implemented.

```
- (void)session:(WCSession *)session
didReceiveMessage:(nonnull NSDictionary<NSString
*,id> *)message replyHandler:(nonnull void
(^)(NSDictionary<NSString *,id> *
_Nonnull))replyHandler
```

```
{
    //TODO: Parse received dictionary

    replyHandler(@{@"Message Status" : ⇥
    @"Received"});
}
```

If the app does not expect a reply handler and includes a `nil` in the `replyHandler` parameter, then it will need to implement the matching delegate callback on the receiving side called `session:didReceiveMessage:`, which looks exactly like the delegate callback above except it does not include a `replyHandler` parameter. This alternative delegate method will be called whenever a `nil` is specified in the reply handler.

Interactive Messaging with Data

Using `NSData` as a transmission medium is nearly identical to the `NSDictionary` approach. This section will only cover the differences between the two methods of interactive messaging transfers.

Whenever using an interactive messaging session to send data, package the transfer data inside of an `NSData` object and then call the `sendMessageData:replyHandler:errorHandler:` method on the `WCSession` singleton, passing in the packaged data object to be transmitted to the recipient app, an optional reply handler block, and an error handler block that will be called in an event of an error during transmission.

Whenever this transfer method is called, the recipient app will get a call to the appropriate `WCSession` delegate method. Similar to the dictionary interactive messaging, there are two methods: one with a reply handler called `session:didReceiveMessageData:replyHandler:` and one without the reply handler called `session:didReceiveMessageData:`. Both delegate methods should be implemented if the app uses the optional reply handler during some transfers, and opts out of using the reply handler for other transfers.

NSURLSession

`NSURLSession`, part of Apple's networking APIs, lets apps use HTTP/S connections to send and fetch data over the network. Since watchOS 2, these APIs have become even more important. That's because starting with watchOS 2, the WatchKit Extension runs on the Apple Watch itself instead of on the phone. This means that whenever the watch is out of range of the paired iPhone the watchOS app can still function as intended, with a few exceptions.

One of those exceptions deals with network requests: as long as `NSURLSession` is being used to perform network operations, then watchOS has the capabilities to connect to a known Wi-Fi access point to perform network tasks. This means watch apps no longer need to be tethered to the paired iPhone in order to access network APIs or upload files to the web. Of course, there's still the concern of what to do when the watch is both untethered and not around any known Wi-Fi access points; ensuring networking errors are properly handled will mitigate this concern.

Summary

In this chapter, you learned all about the new Watch Connectivity Framework provided by watchOS 2 that allows the parent and watch apps to talk to one another to send and receive data that both apps need to function properly.

In addition, you added a new class for the Top 10 app for a singleton WCSession object. Complete this Background File Transfer task in the Going Further section below to store downloaded album artwork on both the watch and iPhone, meaning the app doesn't need to perform duplicate network requests if the artwork had already been downloaded by one of the apps.

With all this knowledge at hand, you're one step closer to making a truly connected WatchKit app by letting the two apps talk to each other in ways that were previously simply not possible.

Going Further

In this chapter, you discovered the Watch Connectivity Framework and all the ways that you can send and receive data using `WCSession` and the associated APIs. For this Going Further section, you'll put your learning to work by adding the following new feature to the Top 10 app:

- On the Watch App, include the Watch Connectivity Framework in the detail view and whenever the watch app makes the request for the album artwork, save the image to the app's documents directory and then transmit the file to the iPhone app. Use the `SessionManager` class that was created at the beginning of this chapter to perform these calls on `WCSession`.
- On the iPhone app, implement `WCSessionDelegate` callbacks in the App Delegate and implement the background file transfer callback delegate to accept and store the received image.

Remember, if you get stuck or need a hint, the completed tutorial is available in the sample code available on the companion website.

Chapter 7: Building Complications with ClockKit

Chapter Overview

Complications are small widgets that appear on the watch face. There are many different styles of complications that users can choose from on the Apple Watch. ClockKit is an API that allows developers to build custom complications bundled with existing watchOS apps. Use of this API can extend apps and provide even more functionality to users.

This chapter will cover the following aspects of ClockKit in detail:

- Background information about how complications work
- Configuring the project for complications
- The available complication types
- Designing content for a complication
- Complication implementation in the sample Top 10 app
- Handling data updates to complications

Throughout the process of learning about complications, we will modify the Top 10 app to add a complication that displays the current top song on the watch face.

How complications work

Apple designed complications such that they could be updated and rendered by watchOS at regular time intervals in order to be more battery efficient. To work within this design constraint, complications are laid out using a timeline metaphor.

The creation of the timeline and the updates are handled through a data manager class that conforms to the `CLKComplicationDataSource` protocol. Through this protocol, watchOS queries the complication to determine what content will be displayed during a given time period throughout the day (Figure 7.1).

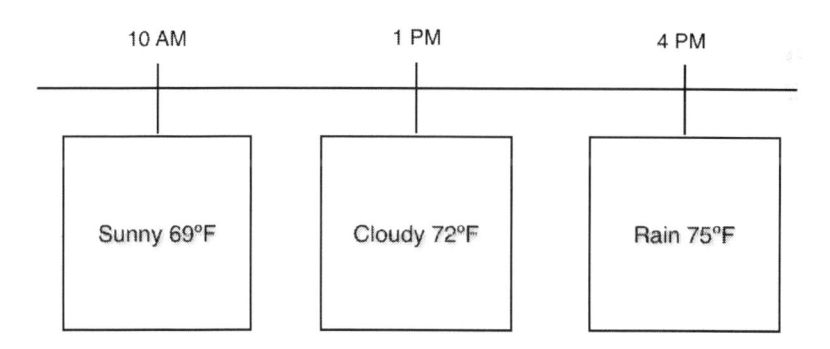

Figure 7.1 – A visual timeline of a complication's data.

The data is always available to watchOS so that as quickly as the user raises their wrist the on-screen updates are completed without having to query third party apps.

Design considerations for complications

WatchOS includes an assortment of watch face styles and complication shapes and sizes for each of the different face styles. While the watch face styles may look very different from one another, they all fall into three types of face families: modular, utilitarian, and circular.

Each of the watch face families contains different types of complications: Modular small, modular large, utilitarian small, utilitarian large, utilitarian small flat, circular small, and extra large (Figure 7.2).

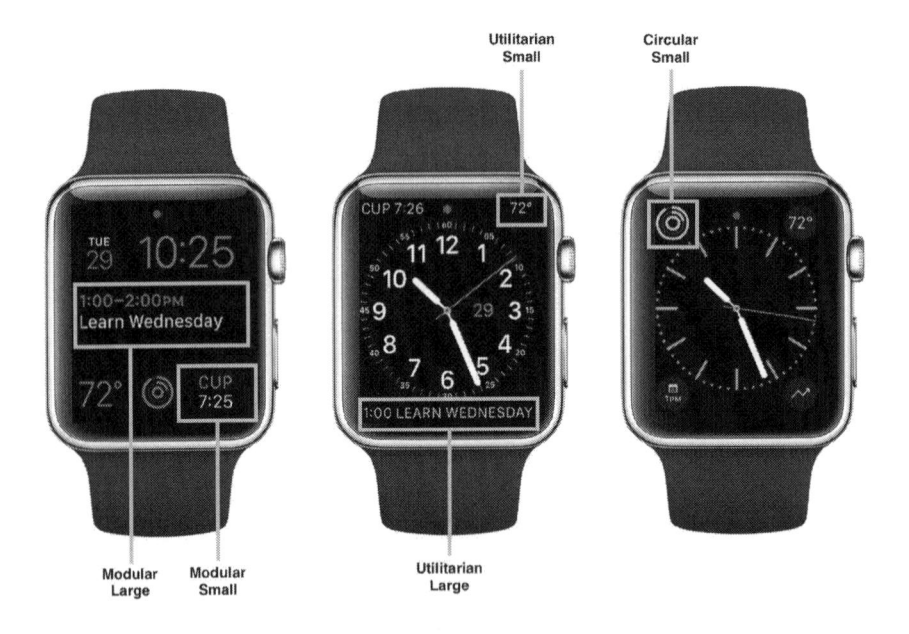

Figure 7.2 – The variations of watch face complications inside of watchOS 2.

Since each complication varies in the amount of data it can visually display, carefully selecting the style of complication is crucial. Only supported complications will appear. We recommend that you try to support all watch complication styles.

Because the text and images in the complication will be colored according to the color set by the user, the complication will be adjusted automatically by watchOS. This means that any images used within complications must be template-based images – only the image alpha channel will be used to define the image contents for display.

Text and images used in complications are not rendered by `WKInterfaceLabel` or `WKInterfaceImage`. Instead, they are rendered by new classes, namely `CLKSimpleTextProvider` and `CLKImageProvider`. You may also use `CLKDateTextProvider` for formatting dates, `CLKRelativeDateTextProvider` for formatting relative dates, and `CLKTimeTextProvider` for working with time-based text. These classes will be covered in detail later in this chapter.

Complications are based on templates, which are defined programmatically using Apple-provided subclasses. The base class for templates is `CLKComplicationTemplate`. Within each of the subclass templates derived from `CLKComplicationTemplate`, there are various elements that each template can handle, such as multi-line text, icons, and more. You should pick the appropriate complication template for the type of data the complication will need to display. In the following sections the various template options available when designing complications are discussed.

Modular

The modular watch face features large readouts and one of the largest areas for displaying text when compared to the other available faces. The modular watch face features both small and large complications.

Modular Large

The Modular Large complications feature a large area that can handle both images and multiple lines of text. There are various templates that work with this family.

`CLKComplicationTemplateModular LargeStandardBody` contains 3 rows of text, a header text provider, body1 text provider, and body2 text provider. There is an optional image provider for an in-line header image.

`CLKComplicationTemplateModularLargeTallBody` contains 2 rows of text, a header text provider, and a body text provider.

`CLKComplicationTemplateModularLargeColumns` contains 2 columns and 3 rows of text in each column, with optional in-line images for each row.

`CLKComplicationTemplateModularLargeTable` contains a header row with 1 column, then a table containing 2 columns and 2 rows for each column of text. There is an optional image provider that places an in-line image in the header row.

Modular Small

Modular Small is a complication family that can feature either images or smaller text elements but cannot handle larger blocks of text.

`CLKComplicationTemplateModularSmallSimpleImage` contains a singular image provider that centers the image inside of the complication.

`CLKComplicationTemplateModularSmallColumnsText` contains 2 columns of text with 2 rows for each column.

`CLKComplicationTemplateModularSmallStackImage` contains a header image on the first row with a text provider below to create a stacked effect.

`CLKComplicationTemplateModularSmallSimpleText` provides a singular text provider that centers its text inside of the complication.

`CLKComplicationTemplateModularSmallStackText` contains two text providers stacked on top of another to create two rows of text.

`CLKComplicationTemplateModularSmallRingImage` provides an inner image provider centered within the complication, with an outer progress ring provided by watchOS to specify a custom value to indicate level of progress.

`CLKComplicationTemplateModularSmallRingText` provides an inner text provider that gets centered within the complication, with an outer progress ring to specify a custom value to indicate level of progress.

Utilitarian

The utilitarian watch face family provides two different styles which are similar to the modular family. The large utilitarian complication, however, only contains a single template; but, the small complications contain similar templates found in the modular family.

Utilitarian Large

`CLKComplicationTemplateUtilitarianLargeFlat` provides a single line containing a text provider and optional in-line image provider to show image before the text.

Utilitarian Small

`CLKComplicationTemplateUtilitarianSmallFlat` provides a single line containing a text provider and optional in-line image provider to show image before the text.

`CLKComplicationTemplateUtilitarianSmallSquare` provides a singular image provider that centers its contents inside of the complication.

`CLKComplicationTemplate UtilitarianSmallRingText` provides an inner text provider that gets centered within the complication, with an outer progress ring to specify a custom value to indicate level of progress.

`CLKComplicationTemplate UtilitarianSmallRingImage` provides an inner image provider that gets centered within the complication, with an outer progress ring to specify a custom value to indicate level of progress.

Circular

The circular family of complications features only one size: small. Because of this, the circular watch face is best used when content can fit inside a smaller area.

`CLKComplicationTemplate CircularSmallSimpleImage` contains a singular image provider that centers its contents inside of the complication.

`CLKComplicationTemplateCircularSmallStackImage` contains a header image on the first row with a text provider below to create a stacked effect.

`CLKComplicationTemplateCircularSmallSimpleText` contains a singular text provider that centers its text inside of the complication.

`CLKComplicationTemplateCircularSmallStackText` contains two text providers stacked on top of each other to create two rows of text.

`CLKComplicationTemplateCircularSmallRingImage` provides an inner image provider centered within the complication, with an outer progress ring to specify a custom value to indicate level of progress.

`CLKComplicationTemplateCircularSmallRingText` provides an inner text provider that gets centered within the complication, with an outer progress ring to specify a custom value to indicate level of progress.

Configuring a project for complications

When you are first creating the project (see Appendix I for the Top 10 app), Xcode offers a checkbox to enable Complication support (Figure 7.3).

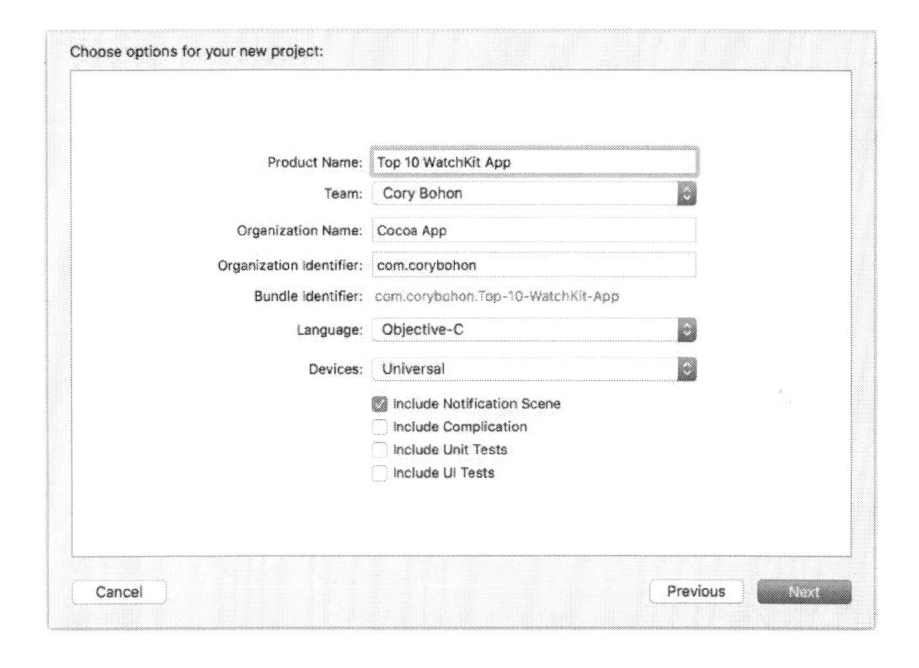

Figure 7.3 – Enabling Complications support is a simple checkbox when initially creating your WatchKit app extension.

By enabling this option, you automatically create a subclass of `NSObject` called `ComplicationController`, which contains the delegate methods already set up and conforming to the `CLKComplicationDataSource` protocol. Each of these methods asks a specific question of the app to determine what content to show in the complication. This will be covered more in depth in the next section.

When you create a WatchKit app without enabling complications, you can still create a new `NSObject` subclass using a custom naming scheme and conforming the class to the `CLKComplicationDataSource` protocol.

Once you have created a class to handle the data source protocol, open the Project settings, select the WatchKit Extension target, and then open the General tab (Figure 7.4) and expand the "Complications Configuration" section.

Once here, ensure that the appropriate Data Source Class has been set. This is the class that watchOS will query to get new data to populate the complication. In addition, this section specifies the configuration families of complications the app will support and sets the group in the `XCAsset` file that contains the images for the complication families.

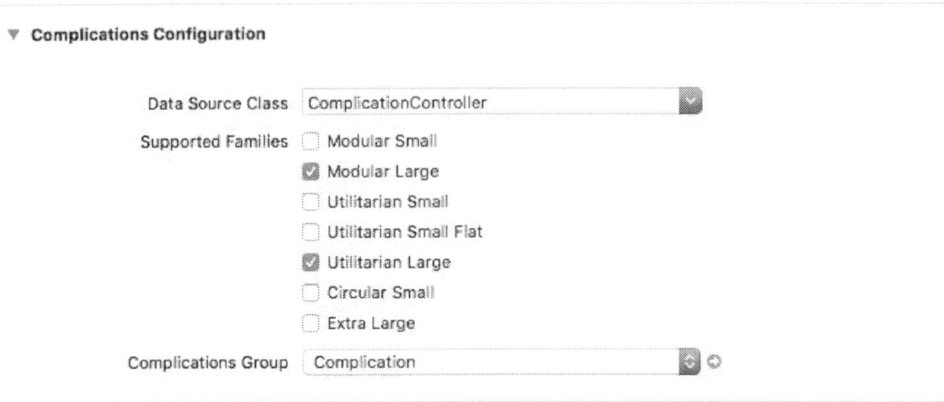

Figure 7.4 – In the target settings set the complication data source class, the types of supported complications, and the asset catalog group that will house any image assets used in the complication.

When you configure the complication support in the Top 10 app, ensure that the class `ComplicationController` is selected in the Data Source Class field and that Modular Large type is the only selected Support Family.

Now that the data controller and supported complication family have been set, you can configure the rest of the complication from within the data source class as explained in the next section.

Implementing a complication

To fully implement a complication, the watch complication data source must conform to the `CLKComplicationDataSource` protocol. This section will explain these delegate methods that must be implemented to properly configure a complication on the watch face.

Supplying Timeline Information

`getSupportedTimeTravelDirectionsForComplication:withHandler:` will be called to specify which directions of Time Travel the complication supports. The method can return `CLKComplicationTimeTravelDirectionNone`, `CLKComplicationTimeTravelDirectionForward`, and/or `CLKComplicationTimeTravelDirectionBackward` to the handler.

`getTimelineStartDateForComplication:withHandler:` is called to determine the earliest date for which the complication will supply data. The method returns an `NSDate` to the handler.

`getTimelineEndDateForComplication:withHandler:` is called to determine the last date for which the complication will supply data. The method returns an `NSDate` to the handler.

Supplying Timeline Entries

`getCurrentTimelineEntryForComplication:withHandler:` method is called to specify the current timeline entry that will be presented on the watch face for the current time. The developer will create a new `CLKComplicationTimelineEntry` object, which gets passed to the handler.

`getTimelineEntriesForComplication:beforeDate:limit:withHandler:` method is called to get timeline events before the passed-in date for backward Time Travel. If there is data to return, the developer will create an `NSArray` of `CLKComplicationTimelineEntry` objects, ensuring no more than the limit value is created, then pass the array to the handler.

`getTimelineEntriesForComplication:afterDate:limit:withHandler:` this method is called to get timeline events after the passed-in date for forward Time Travel. If there is data to return, generate an `NSArray` of `CLKComplicationTimelineEntry` objects, ensuring no more than the limit value is created, then pass the array to the handler.

Whenever timeline entries are specified, watchOS caches them for later and will present entries automatically at the time specified in the `CLKComplicationTimelineEntry` objects.

Time Travel was introduced in watchOS 2, and is a feature that allows the user to roll the Digital Crown forward or backward on the watch face to see upcoming or previous complication entries. However, a complication does not need to support Time Travel, and in the latest versions of watchOS, this feature must be explicitly enabled by the user. If you do not implement the data methods for previous and future data, the complication will fade out whenever the user enters Time Travel mode. Complications can support forward or backward time travel independently of one another.

Responding to Scheduled Updates

The `requestedUpdateDidBegin` method is called whenever the complication has been requested to update its contents either automatically or manually through `CLKComplicationServer`.

The `requestedUpdateBudgetExhausted` method is called whenever the complication's budgetary constraints have been reached for the day and the complication can no longer be updated.

Providing Placeholder Templates

`getPlaceholderTemplateForComplication:withHandler:` is called by watchOS whenever the user installs a watchOS app containing a complication. This method provides placeholder data to the complication whenever the user is configuring complications. It caches the result and is called only once per watch app installation. Beginning with watchOS 3, this method is still available, but is recommended that you utilize the method `getLocalizableSampleTemplateForComplication:withHandler:` instead.

Determining Privacy Behavior

`getPrivacyBehaviorForComplication:withHandler:` is called so that watchOS can determine whether or not the data contained in the complication is security-sensitive. The method should return either `CLKComplicationPrivacyBehaviorShowOnLockScreen` to show content on the lock screen or `CLKComplicationPrivacyBehaviorHideOnLockScreen` to hide content on the lock screen.

To demonstrate how complications work in a real watchOS app, update the Top 10 app to support static data inside of a complication. To begin, open the `ComplicationController` implementation file, and edit the file.

```objc
#import "ComplicationController.h"

@interface ComplicationController ()

@property (nonatomic, strong) NSArray *timelineEntries;

@end

@implementation ComplicationController

- (id)init
{
    if (self = [super init]) {
        self.timelineEntries = @[@"Never Gonna Give You Up
        by Rick Astly", @"Unlock My iPhone by FBI",
        @"The Screen Door Song by Kyle Richter"];
    }
    return self;
}

- (void)requestedUpdateDidBegin
{

}
```

The `requestedUpdateDidBegin` method will be called whenever the complication updates are about to start. Here, the `timelineEntries` property on the complication is populated with static data in the `init` method for ease of demonstration. If this were a deployed app, the data might be pulled from the local data store, or network location.

```objc
#pragma mark - Timeline Configuration
- (void)getSupportedTimeTravelDirectionsForComplication:
(CLKComplication *)complication
withHandler:(void(^)(CLKComplicationTimeTravelDirections
directions))handler
{
    handler(CLKComplicationTimeTravelDirectionForward);
}
```

```objc
- (void)getTimelineStartDateForComplication:
(CLKComplication *)complication withHandler:
(void(^)(NSDate * __nullable date))handler
{
    handler([NSDate date]);
}

- (void)getTimelineEndDateForComplication:
(CLKComplication *)complication withHandler:
(void(^)(NSDate * __nullable date))handler
{
    handler([[NSDate date] dateByAddingTimeInterval:
    6 * 60 * 60]);
}

- (void)getPrivacyBehaviorForComplication:
(CLKComplication *)complication withHandler:
(void(^)(CLKComplicationPrivacyBehavior
privacyBehavior))handler
{
    handler(CLKComplicationPrivacyBehaviorShowOnLockScreen);
}
```

In the previous methods, the complication specifies that it will support the forward Time Travel – again, this feature needs to be explicitly enabled by the user in the Watch app settings. The timeline will start with the current date and end 6 hours from the current date. Lastly, the complication doesn't have any privacy implications and will be shown all the time, even when the Apple Watch is locked.

```objc
#pragma mark - Timeline Population
- (void)getCurrentTimelineEntryForComplication:
(CLKComplication *)complication withHandler:
(void(^)(CLKComplicationTimelineEntry * __nullable))handler
{
    if (complication.family ==
    CLKComplicationFamilyModularLarge)
    {
```

```
        CLKComplicationTimelineEntry *entry = [self ➡
        createTimelineEntryWithHeaderText:@"Top 10" ➡
        bodyText:[self.timelineEntries ➡
         objectAtIndex:0] andDate:[NSDate date]];

        handler(entry);
    }

    handler(nil);
}
```

The `getCurrentTimelineEntryForComplication` will call out to the helper method named `createTimelineEntryWithHeaderText:bodyText:andDate:`, which will return a `CLKComplicationTimelineEntry` object. This timeline object is passed directly into the handler block for the current timeline entry (the entry that should be display first).

```
- (void)getTimelineEntriesForComplication: ➡
(CLKComplication *)complication afterDate:(NSDate *)date➡
limit:(NSUInteger)limit withHandler: ➡
(void (^)(NSArray<CLKComplicationTimelineEntry *> * ➡
_Nullable))handler
{
    if (complication.family != ➡
    CLKComplicationFamilyModularLarge)
    {
        handler(nil);
    }

    NSMutableArray *timelineEntries = ➡
    [[NSMutableArray alloc] init];

    NSDate *dateOffset = ➡
    [date dateByAddingTimeInterval:60 * 60 * 1];

    for (NSString *string in self.timelineEntries)
    {
        [timelineEntries addObject: ➡
        [self createTimelineEntryWithHeaderText:@"Top 10" ➡
```

```
    bodyText:string andDate:dateOffset]];

    dateOffset = [dateOffset dateByAddingTimeInterval: ➡
    60 * 60 * 1];
  }

  handler(timelineEntries);
}
```

For the remainder of the timeline entries, the `getTimelineEntriesForComplication:afterDate:limit:withHandler:` method is called. This protocol method requires that the remainder of the timeline entries after the passed date be packaged into an `NSArray` object and be passed back into the handler block. When implementing this method in an app with live data, extra care should be taken to ensure the limit of the items (defined by the limit value passed into this method) is not exceeded when passing in the array.

```
#pragma mark - Placeholder Templates
- (void) getLocalizableSampleTemplateForComplication: ➡
(CLKComplication *) complication withHandler: ➡
(void(^)(CLKComplicationTemplate * __nullable ➡
complicationTemplate))handler
{
  if (complication.family != ➡
  CLKComplicationFamilyModularLarge) {
      handler(nil);
  }

  CLKComplicationTemplateModularLargeStandardBody ➡
  *modularLarge = ➡
  [[CLKComplicationTemplateModularLargeStandardBody ➡
  alloc]  init];

  modularLarge.headerTextProvider = [CLKSimpleTextProvider ➡
  textProviderWithText:@"Top Song"];

  modularLarge.body1TextProvider = [CLKSimpleTextProvider ➡
  textProviderWithText:@"-"];
```

```
    handler(modularLarge);
}
```

The `getPlaceholderTemplateForComplication:withHandler:` method constructs a single instance of `CLKComplicationTemplateModularLargeStandardBody`, the only complication type supported by this app, and adds faux header and body text before returning the object in the handler block. This object is cached by watchOS and the method will only be queried once per installation of the app. The faux complication template object returned is used by watchOS when users are selecting a complication to display inside of the watch face customization view.

```
#pragma mark - Helper Methods
- (CLKComplicationTimelineEntry *)
createTimelineEntryWithHeaderText:(NSString *)
header bodyText:(NSString *)body andDate:(NSDate *)date
{
    CLKComplicationTemplateModularLargeStandardBody
    *modularLarge =
    [[CLKComplicationTemplateModularLargeStandardBody
     alloc] init];

    modularLarge.headerTextProvider =
    [CLKSimpleTextProvider textProviderWithText:@"Top Song"];

    modularLarge.body1TextProvider =
    [CLKSimpleTextProvider textProviderWithText:body];

    return [CLKComplicationTimelineEntry entryWithDate:date
    complicationTemplate:modularLarge];
}
@end
```

Lastly, `createTimelineEntryWithHeaderText:bodyText:andDate:` is simply a helper method created to construct a single `CLKComplicationTimelineEntry` and return it. This method is called inside of the `getTimelineEntriesForComplication:afterDate:limit:withHandler:` method and constructs all of the complication timeline objects used by the sample app. A `CLKComplicationTimelineEntry` is an object that wraps a complication template object and a date. These objects are used by watchOS to determine what complication entry should be shown at a given time on the watch face. The date passed into the `entryWithDate:complicationTemplate:` constructor method should be the date at which the complication should update and display the passed-in template object.

About Text and Image Providers

The previous example mentioned a `CLKSimpleTextProvider`. When developing custom watch complications, you need an additional object to handle formatting and displaying text inside of the complications.

Many of the text provider subclasses can automatically adjust the content displayed within the complication based on how much space is available and how much data precision is needed.

Take for instance the `CLKSimpleTextProvider`: This object has two methods that can be used for text formatting. The first method is `textProviderWithText:`, and this is the simplest use case where a simple `NSString` can be passed that is shown in the complication. If the text exceeds the available space, then watchOS handles truncating the text in a specific manner.

The second method, named `textProviderWithText:shortText:`, allows for two

`NSString` objects: The first is the longer text, and the second parameter is a short text alternative. If the longer text has exceeded its size constraint limits and will be truncated, then watchOS will automatically switch to displaying the shorter alternative.

`CLKImageProvider` is also available when formatting images for display for complications.

This method of using image and text providers to provide the content to the complications also allows for styling similarities between complications, which makes the watch face much friendlier for users with multiple third and first party apps with complication support.

Handling updates to data

Complication data can quickly become stale, but there are two ways that watchOS apps can easily keep data updated.

In order to update the complication, a new object called `CLKComplicationServer` is used. This singleton object has the following properties:

`activeComplications` returns an `NSArray` containing all of the active complications belonging to the installed app.

`earliestTimeTravelDate` if the complication supports Time Travel, then this `NSDate` is the earliest time that new data should be supplied.

`latestTimeTravelDate` if the complication supports Time Travel, then this `NSDate` is the latest time that new data should be supplied.

There are two ways to keep the content updated using the Complication Server singleton. The first way is to reload the entire complication and have the data source queried again for all of the data. The following code example shows how the full reload is accomplished for all installed complications belonging to the app:

```
for (CLKComplication *complication in ➡
[[CLKComplicationServer sharedInstance] ➡
activeComplications])
{
    [[CLKComplicationServer sharedInstance] ➡
    reloadTimelineForComplication:complication];
}
```

In this example, each active complication is cycled through in order to call the `CLKComplicationServer` method `reloadTimelineForComplication:` to kick off the reload event. There may be multiple variations of the watch app's complications enabled at any given time.

With the method above, all of the cached data is removed, and the data source is re-queried. This should only be done when all of the data stored in the complication needs to be invalidated and rebuilt.

Most often, however, the second way to keep the content updated is more appropriate. Usually, the timeline just needs to be extended to add more information after the last bit already queried. The following code example shows how the complication data timeline can be extended:

```
[[CLKComplicationServer sharedInstance] ➡
extendTimelineForComplication:complication];
```

With this method, watchOS will query the data provider class for the most up-to-date items only, and will then update that item in the complication interface if necessary.

watchOS imposes a daily limit on the amount of calls to the refresh methods for complications. If this hard limit is reached, then calling these update methods will have no further effect. While this rate limit is not published, implementing the `requestedUpdateBudgetExhausted` delegate method will ensure a callback whenever the daily limit has been reached and the complication cannot be updated.

watchOS allows apps to schedule automatic updates to the complication data. To do this, use the delegate method `getNextRequestedUpdateDateWithHandler:`.

```
- (void)getNextRequestedUpdateDateWithHandler:
(void(^)(NSDate * __nullable updateDate))handler
{
    handler([NSDate
    dateWithTimeIntervalSinceNow:60*60*6]);
}
```

In this sample, the data source will request that watchOS update the complication data every 6 hours. Any future `NSDate` object can be passed to the handler and the complication will get updated when the time is reached, assuming the refresh limit for complications hasn't been reached.

Summary

In this chapter, you learned how to design and build a complication for WatchKit apps. Along the way, you used this knowledge to modify the Top 10 app to support custom complications.

Complications can be used to add extra value to your apps and can even be the main way users interact with your app, in the case of weather apps and other information-ingestion apps. If you adopt this technology for your watchOS 2 app, your users can experience even more functionality that is relatively easy to add.

Going Further

In this chapter, you learned about and implemented a Modular Large complication in the Top 10 sample app, but you also learned about the Utilitarian Large complication type. Use your knowledge learned in this chapter to add support for the Utilitarian Large complication type in the complication data class.

Consult the sample code for the complete solution to this Going Further section.

Chapter 8: Accessing the Sensors

Chapter Overview

watchOS provides access to the majority of sensors on the Apple Watch through various API access. The ability to view heart rate data from the heart rate sensor through HealthKit and the ability to view raw accelerometer data from the accelerometer sensors contained in the watch are both accessible to third party developers. These real-world sensors can be used in different ways inside of watchOS apps to provide core functionality in apps, or add additional information for the user.

This chapter covers the following topics:

- Using `CMMotionManager` to access the accelerometer sensors
- Checking for sensor availability
- Capturing raw motion activity
- Accessing heart rate sensor data from HealthKit
- Additional requirements for accessing Health-related data
- Building a Core Motion wrapper class that will serve as a foundation to use the Core Motion API

Accessing Device Sensors

The Core Motion framework that was first made available on iOS 4.0 is also available on watchOS, and it is the main framework to interact with the accelerometer on the watch. While there are still interfaces for gyro, magnetometer, and attitude data, only the accelerometer data is available on the first generation Apple Watch running watchOS 2.

In order to access the accelerometer data available on the device, `CMMotionManager` will be used. This class serves as the main access point between the app and the raw sensor data from the device.

To test which sensors are available, poll the `isAccelerometerAvailable`, `isGyroAvailable`, `isMagnetometerAvailable`, and `isDeviceMotionAvailable` methods on the `CMMotionManager` object. Apps should only create a single `CMMotionManager` instance for use throughout the lifecycle of the app. A singleton will be created to manage the `CMMotionManager` instance.

CMWrapper.h

```objc
#import <Foundation/Foundation.h>
@import CoreMotion;

@interface CMWrapper : NSObject
@property (nonatomic, strong) CMMotionManager *motionManager;
+ (instancetype)shared;
@end
```

CMWrapper.m

```objc
#import "CMWrapper.h"

@implementation CMWrapper

+ (instancetype)shared
{
    static CMWrapper *sharedInstance = nil;
    static dispatch_once_t onceToken;
    dispatch_once(&onceToken, ^{
        sharedInstance = [[self alloc] init];
        [sharedInstance setupWrapper];
    });
    return sharedManager;
```

```
}
- (void)setupWrapper
{
    self.motionManager = [[CMMotionManager alloc] init];

    if ([self.motionManager isAccelerometerAvailable])
    {
        [self.motionManager startAccelerometerUpdates];
        NSLog(@"Accelerometer Available");
    }

    if ([self.motionManager isGyroAvailable])
    {
        [self.motionManager startGyroUpdates];
        NSLog(@"Gyro Available");
    }

    if ([self.motionManager isMagnetometerAvailable])
    {
        [self.motionManager startMagnetometerUpdates];
        NSLog(@"Magnetometer Available");
    }

    if ([self.motionManager isDeviceMotionAvailable])
    {
        [self.motionManager startDeviceMotionUpdates];
        NSLog(@"Device Motion Available");
    }
}

@end
```

This `CMWrapper` class implementation creates and holds onto a single `CMMotionManager` object called `motionManager`. In the `setupWrapper` method, a hardware check is performed to see which sensors are supported.

There are two methods that will provide access to the accelerometer sensor data. The first method is to manually access the data through the `accelerometerData` property on the `CMMotionManager` object.

However, before using the data, they must be monitored by calling `startAccelerometerUpdates` on the `CMMotionManager` object.

```
CMAccelerometerData *aData = [[[CMWrapper shared]
motionManager] accelerometerData];

[self.label setText:[NSString stringWithFormat:
@"X:%f \nY:%f \nZ:%f", aData.acceleration.x,
aData.acceleration.y, aData.acceleration.z]];
```

The units that are returned in the acceleration `struct` (for X, Y, and Z acceleration values) are measured using G-force. With the previous code, the instantaneous values for the X, Y, and Z acceleration are recorded to a label.

The second and the preferred method of access if live acceleration data is needed, is by using an `NSOperationQueue` and block to receive regular callbacks with updated motion data while the app is foregrounded. Using this method of data access is the most efficient and allows for a custom update interval to be set.

The following code example shows the updated `CMWrapper` that supports block-based callbacks.

CMWrapper.h

```
#import <Foundation/Foundation.h>
@import CoreMotion;

@interface CMWrapper : NSObject

+ (CMWrapper *)shared;

- (void)setAccelerometerBlock:(void (^)
(CMAccelerometerData *accel, NSError
*error))accelerometerBlock;

- (void)stopMonitoring;
```

@end

CMWrapper.m

```objc
#import "CMWrapper.h"

@interface CMWrapper()

@property (nonatomic, strong) NSOperationQueue ➡
*operationQueue;

@property (nonatomic, strong) CMMotionManager *motionManager;

@end

@implementation CMWrapper

+ (CMWrapper *)shared
{
    static CMWrapper *sharedManager = nil;
    static dispatch_once_t onceToken;
    dispatch_once(&onceToken, ^{
        sharedManager = [[self alloc] init];
        [sharedManager setupWrapper];
    });
    return sharedManager;
}

- (void)setupWrapper
{
    self.motionManager = [[CMMotionManager alloc] init];
    self.operationQueue = [[NSOperationQueue alloc] init];
}

- (void)setAccelerometerBlock: ➡
(void (^)(CMAccelerometerData *,NSError *))accelerometerBlock
{
    [self.motionManager setAccelerometerUpdateInterval:0.1];

    [self.motionManager startAccelerometerUpdatesToQueue: ➡
        self.operationQueue withHandler:accelerometerBlock];
}

- (void)stopMonitoring
{
    [self.motionManager stopAccelerometerUpdates];
    [self.motionManager stopDeviceMotionUpdates];
```

```
    [self.motionManager stopGyroUpdates];
    [self.motionManager stopMagnetometerUpdates];
}

@end
```

In the previous code example, an `NSOperationQueue` is created to support the callbacks for new accelerometer data. By calling the method `startAccelerometerUpdatesToQueue:withHandler:` and passing in the operation queue and the accelerometer update handler block, the update operation will commence and the block will begin receiving callbacks.

Using the update interval, watchOS and Core Motion will automatically call the handler block until the `stopMonitoring` method is called. To use this `CMWrapper` class to update a label using real time accelerometer data, see the following example.

```
[[CMWrapper shared]
setAccelerometerBlock:^(CMAccelerometerData ➡
*accel, NSError *error)
{
    dispatch_async(dispatch_get_main_queue(), ^{
      [self.label setText:[NSString stringWithFormat: ➡
      @"X: %f \nY:%f \nZ:%f",accel.acceleration.x, ➡
      accel.acceleration.y, accel.acceleration.z]];
    });
}];
```

This example calls `setAccelerometerBlock,` which passes in the block of code that will be executed each time the system retrieves the updated accelerometer data. Anything placed inside this block is executed with each value update, so keep code within the block to a minimum to ensure smooth operation. In the code example above, the new values are simply placed into a label, and the `X`, `Y`, and `Z` acceleration values are updated in real time.

Apps can then interpret this raw acceleration data into any specific data application. When the app is finished using the motion data, a call to `stopAccelerometerUpdates` will cancel future callbacks to the update handler.

Accessing Heart Rate Data

A heart rate sensor is available on the watch, which aids in workout tracking and recording the resting heartrate of the wearer periodically throughout the day. This information is tracked and stored inside of HealthKit.

There are two methods available to access heart rate data. The first is via streaming the live heart rate data through the HealthKit workout feature; the second method is by accessing the historical data.

This section will cover getting the streaming heart rate data from the watch, but if the app requires access to historical data, then information on accessing this data is available in the WWDC 2014 session 203 video located here: https://developer.apple.com/videos/play/wwdc2014-203/ .

Ensure that the provisioning profile and target capabilities are set up to allow HealthKit access – this is accomplished by enabling a switch in the Target | Capabilities tab in Xcode.

The code examples that follow will demonstrate how to set up and access the live heart rate sensor data in a watchOS app.

The first step is to import the HealthKit framework by adding the following line to the top of the header file in the class that will handle the HealthKit access.

```
@import HealthKit;
```

In the class or interface controller, create both a `HKHealthStore` and `HKWorkoutSession` object. Using these two objects will both give the app access to HealthKit and will create a simple workout session that will be used to fetch the live heart rate data from the device.

```objc
HKHealthStore *healthStore = 
[[HKHealthStore alloc] init];

HKWorkoutSession *workoutSession = 
[[HKWorkoutSession alloc] 
initWithActivityType: 
HKWorkoutActivityTypeWalking locationType: 
HKWorkoutSessionLocationTypeUnknown];
```

Next, create a heart rate `HKUnit` object that will be used to configure the HealthKit request later on.

```objc
HKUnit *heartRateUnit = 
[HKUnit unitFromString:@"count/min"];
```

The final part for initial setup is to ensure that the class conforms to the `HKWorkoutSessionDelegate` protocol and then set the delegate to the class that will be receiving the HealthKit delegate callbacks.

```objc
workoutSession.delegate = self;
```

Before continuing further, the app needs to ensure that HealthKit is available on the device and Heart Rate data is available.

```objc
if (![HKHealthStore isHealthDataAvailable] 
|| ![HKQuantityType quantityTypeForIdentifier: 
HKQuantityTypeIdentifierHeartRate])
{
     return; //No HealthKit Heart Rate Data
}
```

Next, create the authorization request for HealthKit, which will prompt the user to allow access to the data stored in HealthKit.

```
NSSet *typesSet =
[NSSet setWithObject:[HKQuantityType
quantityTypeForIdentifier:
HKQuantityTypeIdentifierHeartRate]];


[healthStore
requestAuthorizationToShareTypes:nil
readTypes: typesSet completion:
^(BOOL success, NSError * _Nullable error)
{
    if (error)
    {
            //No HealthKit access, handle error
            return;
    }

    [healthStore
    startWorkoutSession:self.workoutSession];
}];
```

Once completed, it's time to move on to creating the delegate callbacks and ensure they are implemented in the class that will handle the HealthKit data request. Add the delegate methods for `workoutSession:didChangeToState:fromState:date:` and `workoutSession:didFailWithError:`.

#pragma mark - Workout Delegate

```
- (void)workoutSession:
(HKWorkoutSession *)workoutSession
didChangeToState:(HKWorkoutSessionState)toState
```

```objc
fromState:(HKWorkoutSessionState)fromState
date:(NSDate *)date
{
    if (toState == HKWorkoutSessionStateRunning)
    {
        HKQuery *query =
        [self createHeartRateQueryForDate:date];

        if (query) {
           [self.healthStore executeQuery:query];
        } else {
            [self.label
             setText:@"Unable to Start"];
        }
    }

    if (toState == HKWorkoutSessionStateEnded)
    {
        HKQuery *query =
        [self createHeartRateQueryForDate:date];

        if (query) {
            [self.healthStore stopQuery:query];
            [self.label setText:@"Stopped"];
        } else {
            [self.label
             setText:@"Unable to Stop"];
        }
    }
}
```

In the above delegate method, a check is performed to see the current state of the workout session in order to execute a HealthKit store query that will retrieve the heart rate for a particular `NSDate`.

The following method is an error handler method that will be called if an error is encountered while setting up or during the workout session.

```objc
- (void)workoutSession:
(HKWorkoutSession *)workoutSession
didFailWithError:(NSError *)error
{
    NSLog(@"Error: %@",
    error.localizedDescription);
}
```

Finally, there are two additional methods that need to be implemented — one that handles querying HealthKit for the heart rate data and one that updates the label with the new samples returned from HealthKit.

Whenever the delegate method `workoutSession:didChangeToState:fromState:date` gets called, the state is checked to see if the workout is ending or if it is still running. If it is running, then the following method gets called to handle the live heart rate query.

```objc
- (HKAnchoredObjectQuery
*)createHeartRateQueryForDate:(NSDate *)date
{
    HKQuantityType *type = [HKQuantityType
    quantityTypeForIdentifier:
    HKQuantityTypeIdentifierHeartRate];

    HKAnchoredObjectQuery *heartRateQuery =
    [[HKAnchoredObjectQuery alloc]
    initWithType:type predicate:nil
    anchor:HKAnchoredObjectQueryNoAnchor
    limit:HKObjectQueryNoLimit
    resultsHandler:^(HKAnchoredObjectQuery *
    _Nonnull query,
    NSArray<__kindof HKSample *> * _Nullable
```

```objc
    sampleObjects, 
       NSArray<HKDeletedObject *> * _Nullable deletedObjects, 
       HKQueryAnchor * _Nullable newAnchor, NSError * _Nullable error)
    {
       [self updateLabelWithSamples:sampleObjects];
    }];

    heartRateQuery.updateHandler = 
    ^(HKAnchoredObjectQuery * _Nonnull query, 
    NSArray<__kindof HKSample *> * _Nullable 
    sampleObjects, NSArray<HKDeletedObject *> 
    * _Nullable deletedObjects, HKQueryAnchor *
    _Nullable newAnchor, NSError * 
    _Nullable error)
    {
       [self updateLabelWithSamples:sampleObjects];
    };

    return heartRateQuery;
}
```

The previous method works by creating an `HKQuantityType` that will be set to the heart rate type, followed by an `HKAnchoredObjectQuery` that will contain a results handler block containing the sample results queried from HealthKit.

Once the results handler is called, it further calls the following method. This method is used to update a label using the new sample data with the instantaneous heart rate. As the heart rate changes, this method will receive continuous calls with the most up to date heart rate data.

```objc
- (void)updateLabelWithSamples: 
(NSArray *)sampleObjects
{
```

```
    HKQuantitySample *sample = ⇒
    [sampleObjects firstObject];

    NSUInteger rate = [sample.quantity ⇒
    doubleValueForUnit:self.heartRateUnit];

    dispatch_async(dispatch_get_main_queue(), ^{
        [self.label setText: ⇒
        [NSString stringWithFormat:@"%d", rate]];

    });
}
```

With all of this in place, the app can now read the user's heart rate live. If this sample code will be used in a production app a few changes first need to be made. Namely, there should be a way for the user to start and stop the workout session manually. In addition, HealthKit should be implemented in the parent app.

HealthKit Submission Requirements

If the app is using any HealthKit data, such as the heart rate data, a few additional submission requirements are needed.

- If the app uses iCloud, CloudKit, or other online services, it cannot store or harvest user health data retrieved from HealthKit.
- The app cannot use or share HealthKit data with third parties and may not be used for data mining purposes; if it shares this data without the user's direct, explicit consent, then the app will be rejected.
- If the app is used to diagnose, offer treatment advice, or controls hardware that is used to treat a medical condition, then Apple will ask for the regulatory approval documentation prior to approving the app.

It is very important that these guidelines (and any future guidelines posted in the Apple App Store Review Guidelines document) are strictly adhered to when using the HealthKit framework and accessing user health data. The HealthKit platform is a user-centric model that prides itself on user-based control and access, keeping health data as secure as possible and only stored locally on the user's device.

Summary

In this chapter, you learned about the two main sensors on the Apple Watch and how to access and use each of them via the built-in APIs. In addition, you learned about the ins and outs of submitting a HealthKit-related app to the App Store and the submission requirements surrounding access to the user health data.

With this knowledge, you will be able to take advantage of the accelerometer and heart rate data to create your own motion-based apps, or health or fitness app.

Chapter 9: Animation Techniques

Chapter Overview

With each release of watchOS, Apple adds more features to the layout system to allow for more customization of interface elements programmatically. These changes, coupled with a new animation block, allow for easy in-code resizing of elements, including collapsing and expanding `WKInterfaceGroup` objects.

In this chapter the following topics of WatchKit animation will be covered in depth:

- How the new sizing properties on `WKInterfaceObject` subclass objects allow programmatic changes to element sizing
- How to animate changes to interface object properties using the animation API
- How to animate `WKInterfaceTable` changes

Sizing Methods

`WKInterfaceObject` is the base class for nearly all interface objects used in watchOS apps – objects like buttons, labels, and groups. This parent class has gained many new methods that allow for resizing elements. This section covers these new changes in detail.

Manually Changing Overall Width and Height

watchOS 2 introduced the functionality to set both the width and height of interface elements programmatically by calling the `WKInterfaceObject` superclass `setWidth:` and `setHeight:` methods and passing in a `CGFloat`.

These sizing changes can be animated, which will be covered in the next section. It is important to note that if there are changes to the width or height of a `WKInterfaceImage` object, then the content scaling mode of the image will be automatically changed to `UIViewContentModeScaleToFill`.

Setting Relative Width and Height to Container

Sometimes there might be a case where the width and height of a UI element need to be changed relative to its immediate parent container. In this case, there are two new methods available.

Call either the `-setRelativeWidth:withAdjustment:` or the `-setRelativeHeight:withAdjustment:` methods that are available on a `WKInterfaceObject`. Both parameters are `CGFloat` types. The first value can fall between 0.0 and 1.0 to representing the percentage of visual space the object uses, relative to its immediate parent container. The second parameter is an adjustment value in points that adjusts the width or height.

For example, if a label is added to a group that has a width equal to the entire device screen, and the label should take up 75% of that group's width, the following code example can be used.

```
[label setRelativeWidth:0.75
withAdjustment:0.0];
```

Animating Changes to `WKInterfaceObjects`

The sizing methods discussed in the previous section allow for easy resizing of visible elements at runtime and also allow those changes to be animated. In addition to animating those changes, this section also covers the additional animation properties that are available in WatchKit.

On most interface objects the following changes can be animated:

- Opacity
- Width/Height
- Alignment
- Background Color, also available for groups
- Color/tint, also available for template images in `WKInterfaceImage` objects
- Group Insets

Similar to animation on iOS, `animateWithDuration:animations:` is available in WatchKit on `WKInterface` objects.

For example, the following code sample will cause the background color change on a group to animate (note that `self` here is referring to the interface controller that will be handling the animations):

```
[self animateWithDuration:0.33 animations:^{
    [self.group setBackgroundColor: ➡
    [UIColor greenColor]];
}];
```

Once called, this previous code will animate the visible items specified in the animation block over the duration specified as an `NSTimeInterval`.

It is important to note that this method of animation will not animate content changes to an interface object, such as text or image as those items cannot be animated in watchOS. Additionally, if this method is called in a custom notification interface, the animation block will be ignored and the changes will be made without any animation.

The animation method can be called anywhere in the interface controller flow; however, there are two controller flow methods available in for `WKInterfaceControllers`. The `didAppear` method will be called whenever the interface controller has been fully loaded and presented to the user, and `willDisappear` will be called when the interface controller is about to be dismissed from the user's view. These two methods can be used to kick off animations as soon as the user is presented with content in an interface controller, or they can stop or create a new animation whenever the view is about to be dismissed.

Animation Tips

Animations are a relatively new feature of watchOS, and some precautions are needed to ensure that they are not only useful to users, but also that they don't have adverse effects on the app's performance.

Here are just a few tips to keep in mind when creating animations.

If the interface controller will animate items as soon as the view loads and is presented to the user, then use the `didAppear` method in the interface controller to trigger this instead of `willActivate`. Often times the `willActivate` method is called well before the view has been presented to the user, and the animations will not appear to the user because the objects have not yet been displayed.

While using delayed approaches such as timers or Grand Central Dispatch (GCD) techniques to stagger animations, the following must be noted:

- Interface Controllers must be active in order for the animations to be visible.
- Keep the total staggered animation time as short as possible. Reconsider the usefulness of any longer running in a watchOS app since the user's attention span will be very short.
- If starting animations as soon as the views appear to the user, then to speed things up set all of the initial starting values in the Storyboard.

Updating the sizes of elements will cause the entire interface to be laid out again, which can shift other interface elements naturally. If an app has several concurrent or complex animations, this can adversely affect the app's performance. Remember to keep the animations as simple as possible to achieve the effect desired, and to evaluate real-world performance always test the final implement on hardware and not the simulator.

Animating Changes to `WKInterfaceTable`

`WKInterfaceTable` will automatically animate the majority of changes, adapting the kind of subtle animations desired. Using the `insertRowsAtIndex:withRowType:` or `removeRowsAtIndex:` methods will cause the table to animate the addition or subtraction of these additional rows.

Finally, if updating the content of a row (such as hiding or showing content), then the table view will animate these changes.

To better understand how table animations work, update the Top 10 app so that the content of the table animates into view when the user loads the app and after the network processing has been done.

To do this, open the InterfaceController.m file, and tweak the `reloadData` method to look like the following code:

```objc
- (void)reloadData
{
    [[NetworkController sharedNetworkController] 

    retrieveJSONFeedWithCompletionHandler: 
    ^(NSError *error, NSArray *objects) {

        dispatch_async(dispatch_get_main_queue(), ^{
            [self.table insertRowsAtIndexes:[NSIndexSet 

            indexSetWithIndexesInRange: 
            NSMakeRange(0, 10)] withRowType:@"MainRow"];

            for (NSUInteger index = 0; 
            index < self.table.numberOfRows; index ++) {
                MainRow *row = 
                [self.table rowControllerAtIndex:index];

                [row configureWithJSONItem: 
                [objects objectAtIndex:index] atIndex:index];

                [row.image setHidden:NO];
                [row.label setHidden:NO];
            }
        });

        self.jsonItems = objects;

    } forNumberOfItems:10];
}
```

This preceding code will use the `insertRowsAtIndex:withRowType:` method to cause a subtle animation of the blank table rows. Then, by iterating through the rows, the image and label will be populated, and those objects will be animated into view as well. In order for this to work properly, open the Interface.storyboard file and edit the image and label objects in the row controller to be hidden when the interface controller initially loads.

Summary

In this chapter, you learned all about the animation features available for use in your WatchKit apps in watchOS. At this point, through the knowledge gained in this chapter and through examples, you should have a good basic understanding of how to use these animation techniques to add a little extra pizzazz to watchOS apps.

The Top 10 app was also updated in this chapter to take advantage of animations. Through these newly added animations, all of the table rows now animate in while they are being populated in the sample app.

Experimenting with animations and their effects on groups can often provide meaningful animations to users in watchOS apps, in addition to making these apps feel more fluid and polished like iOS apps have come to be known.

Going Further

For this Going Further section, add an animation to InterfaceController.m so that the background color of the view changes from white to black when launching the app. To do this, use the animation methods learned in this chapter and create a new group inside of Interface Builder to accomplish the color change.

Remember that the answers to the Going Further section can always be found in the book's sample source code online.

Chapter 10: Alerts

Chapter Overview

When an app needs to draw a user's attention, when additional actions need to take place, or when requesting additional information from a user, alerts are an essential feature of iOS and watchOS apps.

This chapter demonstrates how to present various alert styles in watchOS, from general alerts, to action sheets, to watchOS-specific "side by side" alerts. The following pages will discuss what alert styles are available to WatchKit apps and how to present them.

In addition, the Top 10 example code will also be updated to support user notification of events through alert modals.

Alerts and Action Sheets

Alerts are the primary method to grab a user's attention in order to communicate errors and unusual conditions that interrupt the app's flow. They also ensure user interaction before the app can proceed. Action sheets do the same but offer up additional options a user can select in order to proceed, perhaps using an alternative flow in the app.

Alerts and action sheets should be used sparingly within iOS and watchOS apps. Not only do they interrupt the user, but they also only add user confusion and aggravation with an app if the message they are trying to communicate is meaningless.

To ensure alerts are not used frivolously and that they don't aggravate users, adhere to the following principles:

- Always create a Cancel button to give the user a way to ignore the actions presented in the alert.
- Choose an alert style based on the use case: There are three alert styles in watchOS (see figure 10.1): alerts, action sheets, and side-by-side alerts.

Alerts communicate errors that the app encounters when performing a user-generated request. Their purpose is to report errors and unusual states to the user. To be in accordance with standard Apple HIG, alerts should not display more than one button.

Action Sheets can be presented to offer up an additional set of options to users while the app is active when immediate user interaction is required. This view allows for multiple option buttons inside the alert.

Side-by-side alerts communicate errors just like standard alerts but offer users two choices for proceeding. They are a limited to two buttons along with a title and message. In accordance with the HIG, the left button should always take on the role of a cancel, allowing the user to dismiss the alert without any action being taken.

| Action Sheet | Alert | Side by Side |

Figure 10.1 – The three alert styles available in watchOS.

Implementing an Alert

All of the alert presentation functionality is baked into every `WKInterfaceController` instance. The following code updates the Top 10 app so that if an error ocurs during the top 10 list retrieval, a retry alert is presented.

Open the InterfaceController.m file and refactor the `reloadData` method to look like the code below.

```objc
#pragma mark - Data Handler
- (void)reloadData
{
    [[NetworkController sharedNetworkController]
    retrieveJSONFeedWithCompletionHandler:
    ^(NSError *error, NSArray *objects)
    {
        dispatch_async(dispatch_get_main_queue(), ^{
            if (error)
              {
                [self presentAlert];
                return;
              }

            [self.table insertRowsAtIndexes:
             [NSIndexSet indexSetWithIndexesInRange:
             NSMakeRange(0, 10)]withRowType:@"MainRow"];

            for (NSUInteger index = 0;
               index < self.table.numberOfRows; index++)
              {
                MainRow *row =
                [self.table rowControllerAtIndex:index];

                [row configureWithJSONItem:
                [objects objectAtIndex:index] atIndex:index];

                [row.image setHidden:NO];
                [row.label setHidden:NO];
              }
        });

        self.jsonItems = objects;

    } forNumberOfItems:10];
}
```

The `reloadData` method adds functionality that will in turn call the networking method `retrieveJSONFeedWithCompletionHandler` on the `NetworkController`, which will return the feed for available Top 10 items. This method is identical to the existing fetch method, with one exception: inside the completion handler block, an `if` statement now checks to see if an error has occurred during the fetch and then calls the `presentAlert` method if necessary.

```
- (void)presentAlert
{
    WKAlertAction *cancelAction =
    [WKAlertAction actionWithTitle:@"Cancel"
        style:WKAlertActionStyleCancel handler:^{}];

    WKAlertAction *retryAction =
    [WKAlertAction actionWithTitle:@"Retry"
        style:WKAlertActionStyleDefault handler:^{
            [self refresh];
        }];

    [self presentAlertControllerWithTitle:nil
     message:@"Top 10 list currently unavailable"
     preferredStyle:WKAlertControllerStyleAlert
     actions:@[cancelAction, retryAction]];
}
```

The `presentAlert` method creates a `WKAlertAction` object, and a second action button is created called "Retry," which has a call to the new `refresh` method in its completion handler.

The presentation of the alert works by passing in `NSString` parameters for the title and alert message, then a style `WKAlertControllerStyle` enum parameter, followed by an array containing the `WKAlertAction` objects created to the `presentAlertControllerWithTitle:message:prefer redStyle:actions:` method available on all `WKInterfaceController` subclasses.

As soon as this method is called, the alert will be presented modally, covering up the presenting `WKInterfaceController`. Take care to ensure the presentation and updates of UI objects always takes place on the main thread.

Unlike iOS, if multiple alerts are presented on watchOS, the old on-screen alert is dismissed to make way for the new alert. Alerts on watchOS will not "stack" in the same manner as they do on iOS.

Summary

In this chapter, you learned all about alerts, the way they look and interact with users on watchOS, and how to implement them in your own apps.

As you learned in this chapter, alerts should always be used sparingly to ensure consistency between apps and alleviate user fatigue from dismissing alerts. Alerts, when used properly, provide a great way to grab a user's attention when issues arise and need user intervention.

Going Further

For this Going Further section, change the alert added to the Top 10 app so that it uses the `WKAlertControllerStyleSideBySideButtonsAlert` style. Note the differences between the side by side style and the standard alert style.

As always, the answers to the Going Further section can be found in the book's sample source code online.

Chapter 11: User Input and Internationalization

Chapter Overview

The Apple Watch isn't just great for consuming content. It can also serve as a convenient method of user input on the go. Text input on the Apple watch is handled through Siri dictation, through pre-defined snippets of text that can be presented to the user, and through emoji selection.

This chapter will cover the following topics concerning user input in depth:

- How to present the user with an input view that allows for emoji, dictation, and Scribble input
- How to offer up app-specific text recommendations in the input view
- How to capture the user input and use it inside the app
- How to start thinking about internationalizing a watchOS app

In addition, a new notes feature will be added to the Top 10 app so users can easily add information about their favorite songs, which will be stored in the app.

About User Input on Apple Watch

The Apple Watch screen is too small for standard user input mechanics traditionally found on iPhone, iPad, and most definitely the Mac. The device, meant to be worn, doesn't have a method to attach a keyboard or the option to display an on-screen keyboard. These limitations present a problem for how to enable users to enter text. This solution is borrowed from iOS, using Siri and voice dictation software.

Using dictation, users can interact with and input data into apps. Apple has built a custom modal interface that can be presented by any `WKInterfaceController` (Figure 12.1), and once presented, this interface will allow users to select pre-defined text snippets, choose a built-in emoji, or dictate a string of text using the built-in microphone on the watch.

Figure 11.1 – The modal interface presented to users when requesting user input.

Capturing User Input

New features can be added to the Top 10 app so users can add a note about a song, have that note stored in `NSUserDefaults`, and load the locally stored note whenever the user returns to the detail view for that song.

Start by configuring the detail view in the Interface.storyboard Storyboard file: drag out a button and label into the interface. Set the title of the button to "Add Note". Select the label and open the Attributes Inspector, then change the lines to "0" (which will expand to fit all of the content) and set its width to "Relative to Container" and the height to "Size To Fit Content."

Now, open the DetailController.m source file, and add the following properties.

```
@property (nonatomic, weak) IBOutlet ➡
WKInterfaceLabel *noteLabel;

@property (nonatomic, strong) JSONItem *item;
```

The `noteLabel` property will be the label in which the user input is displayed. Set the outlet of the label in the Storyboard scene to this property. The `item` is a `JSONItem` obect, where the detail item will be stored.

Add the following line of code to the last line of code in the `awakeWithContext:` method.

```
self.item = detailItem;
```

The preceding code will ensure that the detail item set in the `awakeWithContext` method is available in other methods in the `DetailController` class.

Add the following `didAppear` method in the DetailController.m file.

```
- (void)didAppear {
    [self.noteLabel setText:[[NSUserDefaults ➡
    standardUserDefaults]objectForKey:self.item.songTitle]];
}
```

This method will be called whenever the detail controller appears on screen, and will set the `noteLabel` text to be what the user has previously stored in `NSUserDefaults`. If the user has not stored any text, then the label will be blank.

Now that the groundwork has been laid for note handling, it's time to add the method that will be called when the user taps the Add Note button in the detail controller. After adding the following method, be sure to hook up the action for the Add Note button in the Storyboard.

```objc
#pragma mark - Notes Handling
- (IBAction)addNoteButtonTapped:(id)sender
{
    NSMutableArray *suggestions =
    [[NSMutableArray alloc] init];

    [suggestions addObject:@"Love this song"];
    [suggestions addObject:@"This is a good song"];
    [suggestions addObject:@"Meh"];
    [suggestions addObject:@"Worst. Song. Evar."];

    [self presentTextInputControllerWithSuggestions:
     suggestions allowedInputMode:WKTextInputModeAllowEmoji
     completion:^(NSArray *_Nullable results)
    {
        if (!results.count)
        {
            //Nothing selected, return
            return;
        }

        NSString *input = [results firstObject];

        [self.noteLabel setText:input];

        [[NSUserDefaults standardUserDefaults]
         setObject:input forKey:self.item.songTitle];
    }];
}
```

The first step is to generate an array of `NSString` objects that serve as text suggestions the user will be shown whenever watchOS presents the input modal. Users can then select this text instead of specifying custom input.

Next, call `presentTextInputControllerWithSuggestions:allowedTextInputMode:completion:`, passing in the suggestions array and a `WKTextInputMode` enum to have the input modal displayed to the user.

The input mode determines which input types are available to the user when the modal is presented. Select among `WKTextInputModePlain`, to allow only plain text, `WKTextInputModeAllowEmoji` to allow plain text and emoji, or `WKTextInputModeAllowAnimatedEmoji` to allow plain text, standard emoji, and Apple's animated emoji gifs.

Finally, use the completion block, which takes an `NSArray` object containing the results of the user input. This handler gets called when the user selects suggested text, dictates text, uses Scribble for custom text input, or presses Cancel to close the model.

For the sample project, the app will retrieve the first object and use that as the text input, setting the returned `NSString` value in both the `noteLabel` and `NUserDefaults`.

It is important to note that whenever the completion block is called, the code contained within the block is executed on the main thread, making it easy to update interface elements without having to dispatch to the main thread.

Internationalization

If an app will be distributed to countries other than the United States, then internationalize the app so that users can understand and use the app in their own language and data formats.

While this publication won't go into all the details on internationalization, a watch app will use the same techniques as iOS for internationalization. The following best practices and tips serve as a quick start guide:

- Instead of using string literals, consider using the `NSLocalizedString` macro that is available in both watchOS and iOS to read in a strings file and input the correct, localized string.
- Use the built-in formats for `NSNumberFormatter` whenever formatting numbers to ensure that the values are being formatted to the user's region and locale settings.
- Use the built-in formats for `NSDateFormatter` to ensure that date strings are formatted according to the user's region and locale settings.

For more information on Internationalization and Localization, visit Apple's in-depth guide in the developer documentation, available here: https://developer.apple.com/library/ios/documentation/MacOSX/Conceptual/BPInternational

Summary

In this chapter you learned how to present users with a set of suggested strings, show the standard modal input view, and process the text that users dictate, use Scribble, or select inside of the input view.

Finally, you updated the Top 10 app so that whenever users go into the detail view, they are presented with an "Add Note" button that lets them easily dictate a note, use Scribble, select an emoji, or select some suggested text that will be added to a label and stored for later access.

With all of this in mind, you can now implement apps that take advantage of user input. You should keep in mind, however, that most users would appreciate interfaces that don't singularly rely on text input through dictation as it presents issues when users need to quickly input something in certain environments.

Lastly, you learned a few tips about how to internationalize your app using some of the built-in macros, and formatters in Cocoa.

Going Further

One item that was mentioned in passing in this chapter is that you can use Apple's animated emoji gifs through the input modal. When you allow users to select these animated emojis, your callback block will receive an `NSData` object containing the `UIImage` representation of the gif.

For this Going Further section, add the ability for users to select an animated image and have it presented below the Add Note button. Keep in mind that the user can select an animated emoji, regular emoji, or plain text, so the app must take this into account when displaying data.

Don't forget that you can find the answers to the Going Further section in the book's sample source code online.

Chapter 12: Handoff

Chapter Overview

Handoff, introduced in iOS 8 and macOS 10.10 (Yosemite), is a feature that allows users to resume activities in apps that were initiated on other devices. When Handoff is available to the current foregrounded app, the user will see a small icon of the Handoff-capable app on the lock screen of their iOS device. Swiping upwards on the icon will launch the app, transferring contextual data via Bluetooth or Wi-Fi. Handoff on the Apple watch works in a single direction: from the Apple Watch to a Mac or iOS device. WatchOS cannot currently resume activities from iOS or Mac devices.

This chapter will cover taking advantage of these features in watchOS and iOS apps, allowing activities to be handed off from the watch to the iOS device. The following topics related to Handoff will be covered in depth:

- How Handoff functions between the Apple Watch and iOS devices
- How to implement Handoff in apps
- How to handle Handoff activities

Additionally, you'll learn how to update the Top 10 sample app to use Handoff so users can switch to viewing a top song on their iPhone from the watch version of the app.

How Handoff Works

Handoff allows users to switch between their iOS, macOS, and watchOS devices seamlessly, picking up in-app activities where they left off, by advertising user activities through registering the activity in Info.plist and creating code that uses the `NSUserActivity` class. Keep in mind that Handoff will only work if the iPhone and Apple Watch are connected to the same Wi-Fi network or are currently paired over Bluetooth.

When iOS or macOS detects that an iCloud-connected device is advertising an activity, the icon of the related app will be displayed (if installed) on the Dock of macOS, or in the Lockscreen of the iOS device (figure 12-1). If a user swipes up on the icon on iOS or clicks the icon in the Dock of macOS, the app will be launched, and the activity information will be passed into the App Delegate where the activity can be resumed on their second device.

Figure 12.1 – The Handoff icon in the lower, left-hand corner of the iOS lock screen showing that an app is advertising Handoff information.

Activities can either be web-based (specified with an NSURL and handled by Safari), or app-based (handled by the installed iOS or macOS version of the app). Implementing both types of activities will be discussed in this chapter.

Handoff on iOS and macOS works in both directions, meaning that iOS can hand off its current activity to macOS and vice versa. With watchOS this functionality differs.

Since the watch is more of a consumption device, Apple decided to make Handoff functionality work one-way with watchOS. Because of this, you can Handoff watchOS activities to iOS or macOS, but you cannot Handoff iOS or macOS activities to watchOS.

Registering Activities

When implementing Handoff functionality, the first step is to register the app activities inside of Info.plist. These registered activities will be used by iOS and macOS to determine if the app can resume activities on the secondary device.

Each in-app activity that can be resumed should have its own activity registration. For instance, if there was a Map app, then the app might have an activity for viewing a map location, getting directions, or seeing the detail view of a particular point of interest. Each of these activities should be registered in the versions of the app (iOS or macOS) that support the Handoff feature.

For the Top 10 app there will be only one registered activity. When the user is viewing the details of a particular item, this activity will be advertised to the iOS version of the app.

Because the Apple Watch doesn't support Handoff originating from iOS or macOS, only the iOS version of the Top 10 app needs to register for the Handoff capabilities for the activity. This registration is handled inside the Info.plist file, and allows iOS to easily find apps capable of resuming a specific activity.

Open Info.plist in the iOS Top 10 target and add a new entry, an Array type called "NSUserActivityTypes." Then add a new String entry under it using reverse domain notation, using the end to specify the type of activity it is. For this code sample, use "com.Top10.viewing" for when a user is viewing a particular detail view of a song (Figure 12.2).

▶ Supported interface orientati...		Array	(3 items)
▼ NSUserActivityTypes		Array	(1 item)
Item 0		String	com.Top10.viewing

Figure 12.2 – The Info.plist file showing the NSUserActivityTypes entries.

Once the user activity types have been registered, whenever another version of the app begins broadcasting an activity, then iOS will offer up the Handoff functionality on the user's iOS lock screen.

Broadcasting App-based Activities

Now that the supported resume-able activities have been registered with the recipient app, the watchOS version of the app can begin broadcasting an available registered activity. When the app broadcasts, iOS and macOS devices will notice the change, and will begin offering Handoff actions. iOS and macOS will only offer Handoff on devices that have the version of the app installed that have the same NSUserActivityTypes registered in its Info.plist file.

To begin broadcasting a user activity on the watchOS version of the Top 10 app, open the DetailController.m file in the Top 10 WatchKit Extension, and then add the following line to the `awakeWithContext:` method.

```
[self invalidateUserActivity];
```

This will cause any previously registered and actively broadcasting activities to be invalidated. Ensuring that this is done before beginning a new broadcast will help alleviate issues where Handoff might still be broadcasting a previous activity.

In the `didAppear` method of the Detail Interface Controller, add the following method call.

```
[self updateUserActivity:@"com.Top10.viewing"
userInfo:@{@"object" : self.item.songTitle}
webpageURL:nil];
```

This is a convenience method on `WKInterfaceController` that is unique to watchOS. This method does not require manually creating an `NSUserActivity` object like in iOS; instead, an object is created and then advertised using the supplied activity name as an `NSString` object.

Whenever the code is executed, watchOS begins advertising that the user is currently using the "com.Top10.viewing" activity, and offers up that activity on the user's other devices that have registered that activity.

You have the option to pass in an `NSDictionary` object containing any relevant data that will be passed to the secondary app when the user decides to activate Handoff and continue the activity on another device. For this example, pass in the `songTitle NSString` object that will be used to populate the detail view controller in the iOS app whenever the user activates Handoff.

Because the app should no longer offer Handoff when the user has left the detail controller, implement the `willDisappear` method and call `invalidateUserActivity`.

```
- (void)willDisappear
{
    [self invalidateUserActivity];
}
```

This will ensure that once the user has left the detail view, the Handoff activity is no longer being broadcast and Handoff will not be shown on the user's secondary devices.

Handling and Resuming Activities

The secondary app that receives the Handoff request will need to be ready for receiving data, and will need to implement a new method inside of the App Delegate.

Open AppDelegate.m and add the following method:

```
#pragma mark - Handoff
- (BOOL)application:(UIApplication *)application
continueUserActivity:(NSUserActivity *)userActivity
restorationHandler:(void (^)(NSArray *
_Nullable))restorationHandler
{
    [[NSNotificationCenter defaultCenter]
    postNotificationName:@"com.Top10.viewing"
    object:userActivity];

    return YES;
}
```

This method is called whenever the user activates Handoff in either the app switcher or from the lock screen in iOS. When this method is called, the app will be passed the created `NSUserActivity` object that contains all of the relevant data in order to resume the user's activity.

To keep the example simple for this demo, an `NSNotification` will be posted whenever this call is received, passing in the received `userActivity` object for the `NSNotification` observer to handle.

The `MasterViewController` class will be the observer. The following code will be added to the `viewDidLoad` method in MasterViewController.m.

```
[[NSNotificationCenter defaultCenter]
addObserver:self selector:
@selector(restoreActivity:)
name:@"com.Top10.viewing"
object:nil];
```

The MasterViewController will start observing for notifications from Handoff activities that need to be resumed.

Whenever Handoff requests an activity to be resumed, the following code in the `restoreActivity` method inside of the MasterViewController.m file will be executed.

```
#pragma mark - Handoff
- (void)restoreActivity:(NSNotification *)notification
{
    NSUserActivity *activity = [notification object];

    if ([activity.activityType
    isEqualToString:@"com.Top10.viewing"])
    {
        NSString *matchString =
        [activity.userInfo objectForKey:@"object"];

        for (int index = 0;
        index < [self.objects count]; index++)
        {
            JSONItem *item =
            [self.objects objectAtIndex:index];

            if ([item.songTitle
            isEqualToString:matchString])
            {
                [self.tableView selectRowAtIndexPath:
                [NSIndexPath indexPathForItem:
                index inSection:0]
```

```
            animated:YES
            scrollPosition:UITableViewScrollPositionNone];

            [self performSegueWithIdentifier:
            @"showDetail" sender:nil];

                return;
            }
        }
    }
}
```

This method first gets the `NSUserActivity` object from the `NSNotification` and proceeds to ensure that the "com.Top10.viewing" activity is the method that was called. This is a common check, and the app is responsible for checking which activity was invoked by the user before performing any specific tasks.

Next, the app proceeds first to match the name of the song with the songs that are available in the table view, and finally to select the song and perform a segue with the selected table view item. This is done because the song title was the only identifying information included in the payload from the `NSUserActivity` – depending on the specific needs of the app, this particular setup will need to be changed to ensure that the appropriate data is sent to resume an activity from Handoff.

With these changes in place, the Top 10 app will now respond to users invoking Handoff by viewing the detail item on the watch and then selecting Handoff from the Lockscreen of their iOS device. Once launched, the iOS app will display the same song information in a detail view that was being displayed on the watch.

Broadcasting Web-based Activities

If an app is mainly web-based and does not have an iOS or macOS app counterpart, then the app can still support broadcasting web-based activities. This type of activity will display the Safari icon, and will bypass any code inside the local app. If cross-platform versions of the app aren't available but a webpage containing the same information can be linked to, then this is a great way to provide additional Handoff functionality to users with minimal work.

To begin broadcasting web-based activities via Handoff, there is no activity registration needed in Info.plist; instead, both macOS and iOS will listen for these events and know they need to be handled via Safari.

Add single line of code like the following example.

```
[self updateUserActivity:@"com.Top10.website" ➡
userInfo:nil webpageURL: [NSURL ➡
URLWithString: ➡
@"http://kylesdiscountscreendoors.com"]];
```

The preceding code snippet begins by specifying a user activity (not required to be registered in the Info.plist on web-based Handoff) and then passes the `webpageURL` parameter that is an `NSURL` specifying the web page that will be loaded in the user's web browser when Handoff is activated.

Summary

In this chapter, you read about using Handoff inside of watchOS – from learning how Handoff works from the ground up from both a user and developer standpoint, to learning how to register, broadcast, and react to users invoking the Handoff functionality from their iOS device.

In addition to learning about Handoff, you went hands-on, implementing Handoff support inside the Top 10 WatchKit app and companion iOS app, allowing the demo app to broadcast an activity when a user enters the detail view on the watch app, and letting the iOS app handle showing the detail view when a user invokes Handoff.

With this knowledge, you can now build sophisticated apps that use the power of Handoff to enable users to continue working on tasks, regardless of which device they are currently using.

Going Further

In this chapter, you also learned about how to implement web-based activities, enabling a user to invoke Handoff and delve straight into Safari through a web URL. For this Going Further section, you'll implement one of these web-based activities.

Add this new activity in the main InterfaceController.m file of the watch app, and ensure that the new activity, when invoked, will open the following URL in Safari:

https://www.apple.com/itunes/charts/songs/

This URL contains the full listing of top songs available on iTunes on the Apple website and is available from the web browser.

If you get stuck on this Going Further section, you can view the completed tutorial inside the sample code available from the book's companion website.

Chapter 13: Building Dock-compatible watchOS Apps

Chapter Overview

Watch apps should be glance-able so users can easily get the information they need with a single look. Apple has made this easy through the Dock on the watch, which is similar to the App Switcher on iOS. In the Dock, apps can provide a single, non-scrolling interface controller full of information that can be updated through either background updates, push notifications, or a combination of both.

This chapter will cover the following topics about making apps available to users in the Dock:

- Ensuring that docked apps are fast to launch
- Keeping the docked app current with snapshots
- Scheduling and reacting to background snapshot updates

This chapter provides an in-depth discussion of techniques on ensure that docked apps are useful to users and that they provide content without requiring the user to open the app.

About the Dock
The Dock is accessible to users by depressing the Side Button below the Digital Crown on the watch once. (Note that depressing the side button twice will activate Apple Pay). This button activates the Dock and displays a list of recently launched apps. To activate the Dock in

the watchOS Simulator, select Hardware | Side Button (or press Shift + Command + B).

By default, the Dock displays the last apps used; however, apps can also be pinned to the Dock so that they're always available. These pinned apps can be added by first launching the app from the watchOS home screen, then opening the Dock to view the "Keep in Dock" button (Figure 13.1).

Apps that are displayed in the Dock are not actually running, but have the appearance that they are. This is done through snapshots of the content and the fact that watchOS can resume apps just like iOS – when the user taps on a docked app, it resumes almost immediately.

Figure 13.1 – Tap the "Keep in Dock" button to pin the app to the Dock. Users can pin multiple apps to the Dock.

Docked apps provide users with an easy-to-view summary of the most important information from the app. Tapping on any of the Docked apps will launch the full app, loading the app.

Making Apps Dockable

Without any additional effort, apps can be docked in the watchOS Dock, but there are some design paradigms that can make the user experience of the apps better when placed in the Dock.

Most Important Elements First

Users need to be able to get information from an app with minimal wait time, including navigation time. If the most important pieces of information in an app is multiple levels deep in a navigation hierarchy, then there should be some view refactoring done to ensure the most important feature(s) of the app is surfaced to the first interface controller presented when the app launches.

Actionable Items

Watch apps are meant to provide actionable items, and Docked apps are no exception. They should provide users with quick, actionable context for items that the user might want to perform in the full app, or through Handoff on the connected iOS device. Keep this in mind when designing for the Dock.

Responsiveness

There are multiple ways that apps can ensure a responsive experience, and a lot of that boils down to ensuring that the data the user will need will be there when they launch the app. This can be accomplished through app background refresh just like on iOS, or through the Watch Connectivity Framework (see Chapter 6 "The Watch Connectivity Framework") to pre-load data in anticipation of a user performing an action or loading a certain interface controller on the watch.

Making New Snapshots

Docked apps give the appearance that they are living apps, constantly updating with information from the Internet, from the full app, or from the companion iOS app. This is done through Background App Refresh; regardless of whether the developer has adopted app refresh technology, so long as the app is being used as a favorite. Favorite apps are those pinned to the Dock, or added to the watch face as a Complication.

These favorite apps are automatically kept in memory and are quicker to launch than other apps. When the Dock is displayed, the app is not actually running; instead a "Snapshot" is displayed. The snapshot is the state of the app when it was last suspended, which may or may not be the current state if the app has been updating in the background from background refresh, or if the data has changed behind the scenes. The snapshot will automatically be updated whenever the user settles on an app in the Dock. However, in the time between when the user settles on an app, the app gets resumed, and a new snapshot is made, the old content will be displayed, which can be a bit jarring for the user.

Fortunately, there is a way to update this snapshot in the background so that what is displayed to the user in the Dock is always the most up-to-date information.

There are five automatic snapshot updates that will happen throughout normal app use without any further integration:

- Suspending the app will cause a new snapshot to be taken since the user has most likely caused information to update in the app by launching it. This new snapshot is scheduled by the system shortly after the user suspends the watchOS app.
- A push notification arriving, combined with the user taking a long look at the notification, will update the app's snapshot to be updated because there is most likely new information inside of the app.
- A complication owned by the app gets updated on the watch face, this will trigger a new snapshot update.
- When the Apple Watch starts up, apps pinned to the Dock will automatically get a new snapshot taken for the new session.

- One hour after the last interaction with the app, a new snapshot will automatically be generated.

The above automatic updates will not hinder any app-scheduled requests for updates, and are merely "in addition to" the updates that the app can scheduled to update the snapshot in the Dock.

Scheduling snapshot updates is done using a Background Refresh API called `WKSnapshotRefreshBackgroundTask`. An example of scheduling this can be seen in the following code example:

```
[[WKExtension sharedExtension]
scheduleSnapshotRefreshWithPreferredDate:
[NSDate date] userInfo:nil
scheduledCompletion:^(NSError * _Nullable error) {
        //Completion handler here
}];
```

Whenever a scheduled snapshot is executed, the `ExtensionDelegate` method `handleBackgroundTasks` will get called when it's time to handle the background task. For the `WKSnapshotRefreshBackgroundTask` type, it may be necessary to ensure the topmost view controller is on-screen and has been populated.

Following is an example of the handleBackgroundTasks method from the ExtensionDelegate:

```
- (void)handleBackgroundTasks:
(NSSet<WKRefreshBackgroundTask *> *)backgroundTasks
{
    for (WKSnapshotRefreshBackgroundTask *task
    in backgroundTasks)
    {
        // Do any pre-snapshot setup here
```

```
        NSDate *newDate = ⇒
        [NSDate dateWithTimeIntervalSinceNow:3600];

        [task setTaskCompletedWithDefaultStateRestored:YES ⇒
        estimatedSnapshotExpiration:newDate ⇒
        userInfo:nil];
    }
}
```

It is important to keep in mind that Background Refresh APIs, while powerful, are budgeted by watchOS to ensure the OS runs smoothly and are fair to all apps on the system that need background refresh support.

It is also important to return from the method by calling `setTaskCompletedWithDefaultStateRestored:estimatedSnapshotExpiration:userInfo`. If this method isn't called within the allotted time, then the watchOS extension will be suspended by the system as soon as the allotted time expires.

Summary

This chapter explained the concepts surrounding the Dock in watchOS, scheduling background snapshot updates of the interface for the Dock, and the various ways that automatic snapshots are created by watchOS.

The Dock is a very powerful feature of watchOS that can ensure that users have instant access to apps, and immediate launch into in-memory apps without any delay or re-loading data. This, coupled with background data fetching and smartly implemented Watch Connectivity will mean that users never have to wait for app data to load.

Going Further

The sample app for this publication can be docked and information displayed to the user about the current top song. For this going further section, update the app so that when the app updates the snapshot, only the initial interface controller is displayed in the snapshot.

Chapter 14: Distributing WatchKit Apps

Chapter Overview

Writing a great watchOS app doesn't mean much without making it available to the public. This chapter will cover the ins and outs of how to prepare an app for the App Store.

In particular, this chapter will discuss the following techniques:

- How to provision WatchKit apps
- How to set version and build numbers for the WatchKit app and extension
- How to generate an IPA file containing the parent iOS app and WatchKit extension
- How to upload and prepare the app for the App Store review process
- How to prepare additional assets that are required, including screenshots and icons

iOS Provisioning

Similar to iOS apps, WatchKit apps and their associated extensions also require provisioning. This means that three profiles must be generated: one for the iOS parent app, one for the WatchKit App, and finally one for the WatchKit extension.

Managing these profiles can be tedious, but fortunately, Xcode can automatically generate and assign the provisioning profiles to all of the targets in a project.

Sign into a developer account in the Xcode settings by following these steps:

1. Open Xcode | Preferences
2. Navigate to the Accounts tab
3. Click the "+" button below the Apple IDs / Repositories listing and select "Add Apple ID..."
4. Sign in with your Apple ID account credentials (Figure 14.1)

Figure 14.1 – Signing into a developer account will give Xcode the ability to create application IDs, signing certificates, and profiles automatically.

Next, ensure the targets are provisioned and signed correctly by Xcode, and configure each of the three targets in the project. Follow these steps for the iOS, WatchKit Extension, and WatchKit App targets:

1. Click the project name in the Project Navigator sidebar
2. Select a target in the project and targets list sidebar
3. Navigate to the General tab, locate the Team drop-down menu, and select the iOS developer account from this list
4. Navigate to the Build Settings tab, and locate the "Code Signing" section
5. Set the value for "Code Signing Identity" to "iOS Developer"
6. Set the value for "Provisioning Profile" to "Automatic" (Figure 14.2)

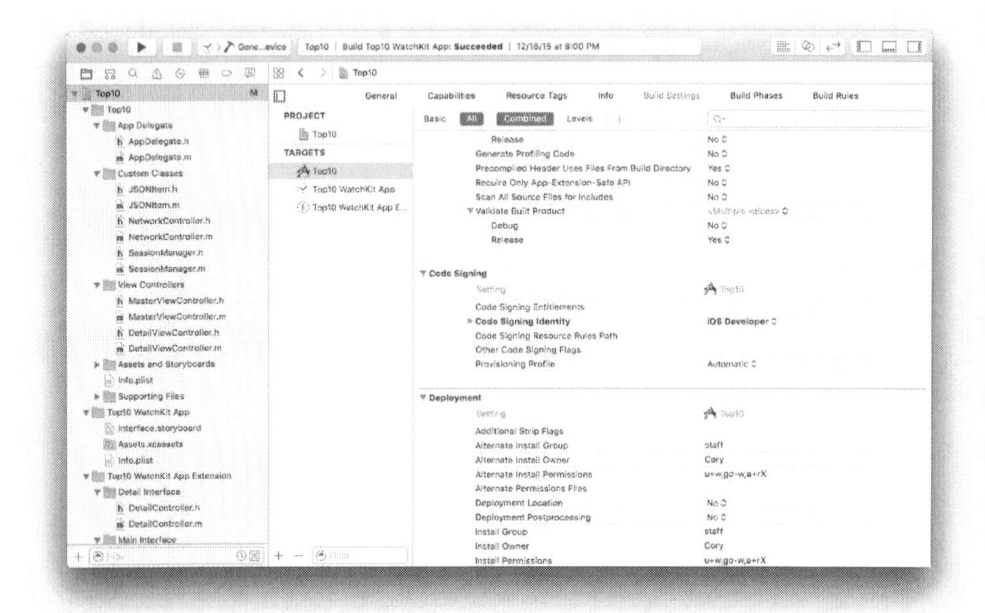

Figure 14.2 – For automatic signing and provisioning of apps by Xcode, these values should be set in the Build Settings tab for the "Code Signing" options.

With these settings in place, Xcode will now be able to automatically configure, generate profiles for, and sign the apps for development and distribution needs without manual generation and configuration of profiles from an Apple Developer account.

To configure apps using the manual method, generating App IDs and Profiles for each of the targets (one profile for development, one for App Store) is required first. Assign those profiles to the targets manually under the Build Settings.

Build Numbers

Because the WatchKit app is basically an extension of the iOS app, it is only fitting that both targets share the same version and build numbers. This is an iTunes Connect requirement, and attempting to submit an app that includes a WatchKit extension with different build numbers will result in an iTunes Connect submission error stating that the version and build numbers for the app and extension must match.

Fortunately, the task of assigning matching version and build numbers can be automated using build scripts in Xcode (explained in the section below). For now, just manually increase the build and version numbers using these steps:

1. Click on the Project file in the Xcode Project Explorer sidebar
2. Select the iOS target in the sidebar target and note the version and build numbers that are currently set on the target
3. Select the WatchKit App target and input the same build and version numbers that were set on the iOS target (Figure 14.3)
4. Repeat this step for the WatchKit Extension target, and any other extensions that may be embedded in the parent iOS app

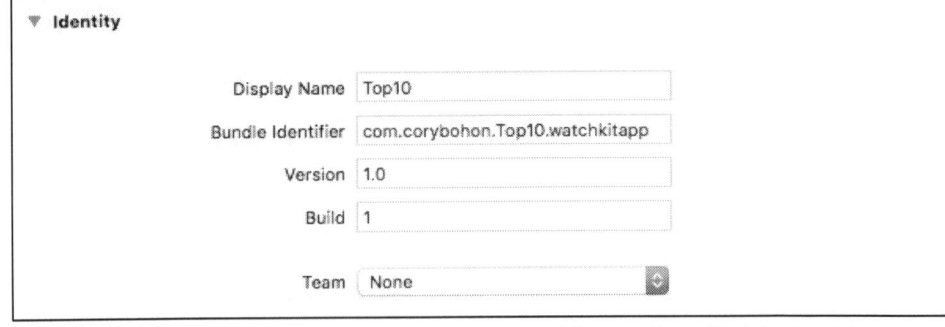

Display Name	Top10
Bundle Identifier	com.corybohon.Top10.watchkitapp
Version	1.0
Build	1
Team	None

Figure 14.3 – Shows the version and build number fields inside of the WatchKit App target of the sample Xcode project.

Note that iTunes Connect requires that version numbers be incremented for each subsequent App Store release, and the build number must be incremented for each subsequent TestFlight beta release.

Generating an Archive Build

Once you have set up Xcode to automatically provision and sign the app and its extension, it becomes easier to generate an IPA (an iOS app archive file) to send to the App Store for review and publication.

To generate an IPA of the iOS app you first need to create an Xcode archive that includes the WatchKit extension. Follow these steps to generate an archive:

1. In Xcode with the project opened, select the iOS app target from the scheme list, and select "Generic iOS Device" as the device to build for (Figure 14.4)
2. Select Build | Archive from the menu bar in Xcode.

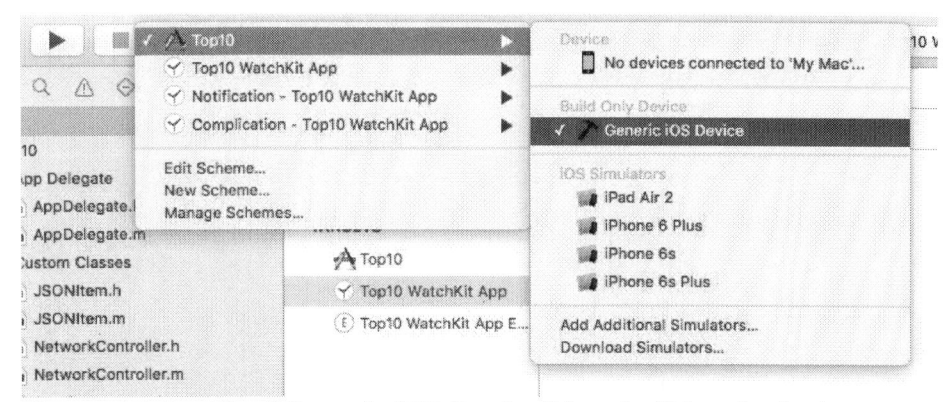

Figure 14.4 – The "Generic iOS Device" is a build-only device created in Xcode 7 to give developers an easier way to build against target devices for archive builds.

Once completed, the Xcode Organizer will open with the current archive build selected.

Create and upload an IPA to iTunes Connect

With an archive build created, there is only one additional step in Xcode to upload the app to iTunes Connect, where it will be evaluated by the App Store reviewers: generate and upload the IPA for the app. Note that this step assumes the app record has already been created in iTunes Connect and is prepared for upload.

For more information on the process of creating app records in iTunes Connect, view the latest documentation from iTunes Connect, https://itunespartner.apple.com/en/apps/overview.

Now that the Xcode archive has been created, build an IPA file and upload the binary to iTunes Connect by taking these steps:

1. Open Xcode | Window | Organizer
2. Select the new Archive Build, then select the blue "Upload to App Store…" button
3. When prompted, select the development team to use for provisioning and signing

4. After a few minutes, a screen shows the data that will be sent to Apple; click the Upload button to begin the submission process (Figure 14.5).

Figure 14.5 – The IPA being sent to iTunes Connect and its contained extensions.

During this process, the IPA file will be generated locally in a temporary location, and will be uploaded to iTunes Connect directly from Xcode. The generated IPA file will include the watchOS extension and app, along with the necessary signing entitlements.

Once the upload is finished, a message will appear stating the submission to iTunes Connect has been completed. In some rare cases, detailed error message may appear, explaining any issues and why the app could not be delivered. Use the error messages to correct any warnings, and then re-try.

iTunes Connect Required Assets

iTunes Connect has a few requirements (Figure 14.6) for assets to include upon submitting an app for review. These assets are similar to those required for iOS apps.

Icon – An Apple Watch icon in JPEG or PNG format, 1024 x 1024 pixels in dimensions, with a minimum resolution of 72 DPI using the RGB color space. This is the icon that will be displayed in the Watch App Store listing. This icon cannot contain rounded corners or layers.

Screenshots – Screenshots that have been flattened with no transparency, in either JPEG or PNG format at 72 DPI resolution. The required screenshot dimensions are 312 x 390 pixels in portrait orientation.

Support URLs – URLs for app support as well as a marketing URL for a website where users can learn more about the app. These URLs will be included in the App Store listing for the Apple Watch app.

Description – A text description of the app that includes details of the features and functionality. This information will be included in the App Store description for the Apple Watch app.

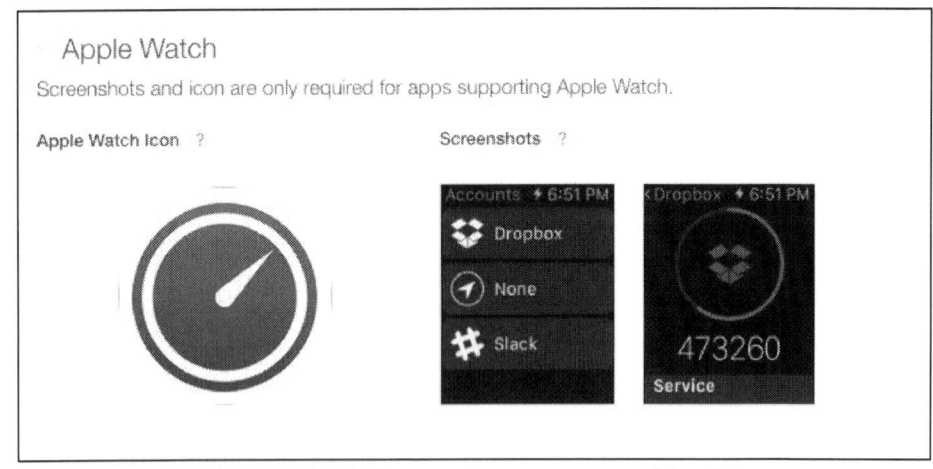

Figure 14.6 – Shows the information requested by iTunes Connect when submitting an iOS and WatchKit app for review.

Automatically Incrementing Build Numbers in Xcode

Xcode includes the ability to add build scripts that will automatically increment the build numbers when building the app. This can help when you need to update multiple build numbers in parallel – in fact, the tool will automatically increment all targets in the same Xcode project without any intervention. This is important since, as mentioned above, the App Store submission process requires all embedded targets to have the same version and build numbers.

Automatically incrementing the build numbers using the Apple-sanctioned method below requires that a Mac with the Xcode Command Line tools installed. Download and install these tools from this developer portal page: http://developer.apple.com/downloads.

To add this feature to your iOS, WatchKit App, and WatchKit Extension, follow these steps:

1. Open the project settings and select the iOS app target
2. Select the Build Settings tab at the top of the view
3. Locate the build number value for the "Current Project Version" field. If the project already has an incremented build number, then set the number to the next build number that will be used. Also ensure the Versioning System value is set to "Apple Generic"

Repeat these steps for the WatchKit app and WatchKit extension targets, using the same value set as the iOS app (Figure 14.7).

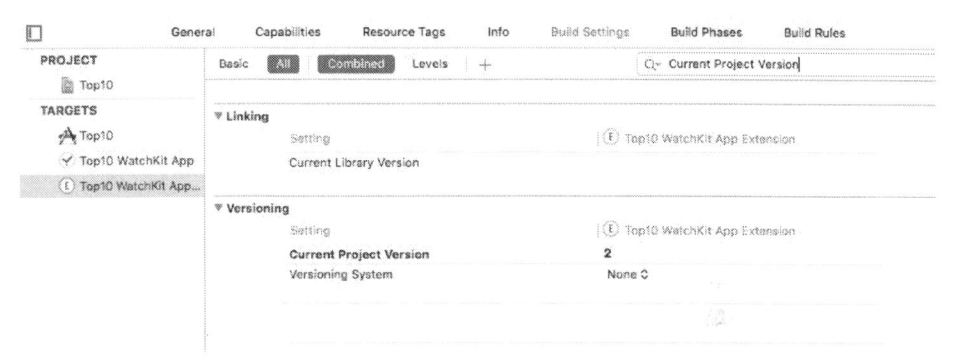

Figure 14.7 – Build settings showing the value placement for "Current Project Version."

Now that Xcode has been set up with the current version number, a script needs to be added in order to make the build numbers automatically increment by one. To do this, open the Build Phases tab for the iOS target and select the Plus button (+) and then "New Run Script Phase."

A new field will appear (Figure 14.8). Add the following shell script to the run script phase in the text area provided by Xcode:

```
config="Release"
if [ "$config" = "${CONFIGURATION}" ]; then
    xcrun agvtool next-version -all
fi
```

This script uses the `agvtool` command line application provided by Xcode to automatically increment the build numbers when running, but only when the app is building in Release mode. The release build will use the current version number, and this command will automatically increment to the next number when archiving.

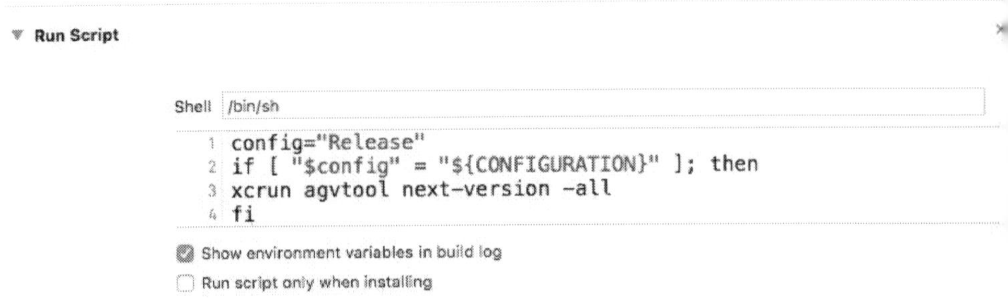

Figure 14.8 – Build settings showing the value placement for "Current Project Version."

Summary

In this chapter, you learned all about how you can distribute your app to the App Store and get your app out into the hands of millions of potential users. This process doesn't deviate too much from the standard iOS app submission process, but as you've seen in this chapter, it does have its own quirks.

With the knowledge gained in the chapter about generating provisioning profiles, setting the build numbers, then generating and uploading your app to iTunes Connect, you are now ready to have your app reviewed and made available to all of your waiting customers.

Going Further

In this chapter, you learned about the command line tool called `agvtool` included with Xcode that can automatically increment build numbers for targets without any intervention by the developer. For this Going Further section, add this functionality to the Top 10 sample app, and build and run the project, then create an archive build of the iOS project to see how the script works and get a feel for the automatic build number system included with Xcode.

Remember that the answers to the Going Further section can be found in the book's sample source code online.

Appendix I: Building the Sample App

Appendix Overview

In this appendix the sample app used throughout this publication to teach various development techniques and explain the features of WatchKit will be covered in depth. While this publication can be used as a general reference, many examples use the sample app as the base project.

For the sample project, an iOS app and a native watchOS app will be created that performs the following tasks.

- Download and parse the iTunes Store JSON feed to gather the top 10 songs on the music charts.
- The iOS app will display a master list of the top 10 songs, with a detail view for viewing the details of each item.

Throughout the publication, additional features will be added to showcase topic-specific technologies throughout the chapters.

Xcode Version Required for WatchKit Development

watchOS requires the WatchKit SDK, which is included with the latest versions of Xcode. Before proceeding with the example code, ensure that Xcode 8 or later is installed.

Creating the Sample Project

Begin by opening Xcode and selecting File | New | New Project. When prompted to select a template, choose the iOS Master-Detail template, it contains the view controllers and Storyboard pre-configured for the exact style project that will be built, one that involves both a master table view and a detail view showing more information based on the master table view selection.

Writing the Networking Code

The networking code that handles the request to the iTunes Store will need to be created – both an object (JSONItem) and a utility class (NetworkController) will be created in order to facilitate the network handling in the sample app.

Create a new file in Xcode using an `NSObject` subclass called "JSONItem." This class will hold the attributes from the JSON feed for each of the songs returned.

The following sample code is the header interface (in JSONItem.h) that should be implemented.

```
#import <Foundation/Foundation.h>

@interface JSONItem : NSObject

@property (nonatomic, strong) NSString *songTitle;

@property (nonatomic, strong) NSString ➡
*artistName;

@property (nonatomic, strong) NSString *albumName;

@property (nonatomic, strong) NSString ➡
*genreTitle;

@property (nonatomic, strong) NSString ➡
*priceInUSD;

@property (nonatomic, strong) NSString ➡
```

```
    *releaseDate;
```

@end

The properties in `JSONItem` will store the song title, artist name, album name, genre of the media, price, and release date.

Now that a class has been constructed to hold the JSON feed data for each song, a new `NSObject` subclass will be created to add networking functionality, called `NetworkController`.

This class will be responsible for making the network request, parsing the JSON feed, and returning `JSONItem` objects for display in the iPhone and Watch user interface. This class will use a singleton pattern.

The following sample code shows the header interface for NetworkController.h.

```
#import <Foundation/Foundation.h>

@class JSONItem;

@interface NetworkController : NSObject

+ (instancetype)sharedNetworkController;

- (void)retrieveTopSong:
(void(^)(NSError *error, JSONItem *topSong))
completionHandler;

- (void)retrieveJSONFeedWithCompletionHandler:
(void(^)(NSError *error, NSArray
*objects))completionHandler forNumberOfItems:
(NSUInteger)numberOfSongs;

@end
```

The methods included with the header take a completionHandler that will be handed either a `JSONItem`, or an array of `JSONItem` objects.

Below is the implementation code for NetworkController.m. Make edits to this file to include the additions for network handling.

```objc
@interface NetworkController ()
@property (nonatomic, strong) NSURLSession ➡ *session;

@end

@implementation NetworkController

+ (instancetype)sharedNetworkController
{
    static NetworkController *sharedManager = nil;
    static dispatch_once_t onceToken;
    dispatch_once(&onceToken, ^{
        sharedManager = [[self alloc] init];
        [sharedManager setupBaseSession];
    });

    return sharedManager;
}

#pragma mark - Internal Setup
- (void)setupBaseSession
{
    NSURLSessionConfiguration *sessionConfig = ➡ [NSURLSessionConfiguration ➡ defaultSessionConfiguration];

    [sessionConfig setHTTPAdditionalHeaders: ➡ @{@"Content-Type" : @"application/json", ➡ @"Accept" : @"application/json"}];
```

```objc
    self.session = [NSURLSession 
    sessionWithConfiguration:sessionConfig];
}

#pragma mark - Methods
- (void)retrieveTopSong: 
(void(^)(NSError *error, JSONItem *topSong)) 
completionHandler
{
    [self 
    retrieveJSONFeedWithCompletionHandler: 
    ^(NSError *error, NSArray *objects) {

        if (!error && completionHandler)
        {
            completionHandler (nil, 
            [objects firstObject]);
        }

    } forNumberOfItems:1];
}

- (void)retrieveJSONFeedWithCompletionHandler: 
(void(^)(NSError *error, NSArray 
*objects))completionHandler 
forNumberOfItems:(NSUInteger)numberOfSongs
{
    NSMutableURLRequest *request = 
    [NSMutableURLRequest requestWithURL: 
    [NSURL URLWithString:[NSString 
    stringWithFormat: 
    @"https://itunes.apple.com/us/rss/topsongs/ 
    limit=%lu/json", numberOfSongs]]];

    [request setHTTPMethod:@"GET"];

    NSURLSession *session = [self session];
```

```objc
NSURLSessionTask *requestTask =
[session dataTaskWithRequest:request
completionHandler:
^(NSData *data, NSURLResponse *response,
NSError *error) {

    NSHTTPURLResponse *httpResponse =
    (NSHTTPURLResponse *)response;

     if (error ||
     (httpResponse.statusCode != 200))
      {
        NSError *error =
        [NSError errorWithDomain:
         @"com.watchkit.test" code:300
         userInfo:@{NSLocalizedDescriptionKey
         : @"Error retrieving JSON feed."}];

        if (completionHandler) {
          completionHandler (error, nil);
        }
     }

     __autoreleasing NSError *jsonResponseError;
    NSDictionary *jsonResponse =
    [NSJSONSerialization JSONObjectWithData:data
    options:0 error:&jsonResponseError];

    NSMutableArray *arrayToReturn =
    [[NSMutableArray alloc] init];

    if (numberOfSongs == 1) {
        [NSDictionary *dictionary =
        jsonResponse[@"feed"][@"entry"];

        [[arrayToReturn addObject:
```

```objc
                    [self itemForDictionary:dictionary]];
            } else {
                for (NSDictionary *dictionary in ➡
                jsonResponse[@"feed"][@"entry"]) {
                    [arrayToReturn addObject: ➡
                    [self itemForDictionary:dictionary]];
                }
            }

        if (completionHandler) {
            completionHandler(nil, arrayToReturn);
        }

    }];
    [requestTask resume];
}

- (JSONItem *)itemForDictionary: ➡
(NSDictionary *)dictionary
{
    JSONItem *item = [[JSONItem alloc] init];

    item.artistName = ➡
    dictionary[@"im:artist"][@"label"];

    item.albumName = ➡
    dictionary[@"im:collection"][@"im:name"]➡
    [@"label"];

    item.songTitle = ➡
    dictionary[@"im:name"][@"label"];

    item.releaseDate = ➡
    dictionary[@"im:releaseDate"][@"attributes"]➡
    [@"label"];

    item.genreTitle = ➡
    dictionary[@"category"][@"attributes"]➡
```

```
        [@"label"];

        item.priceInUSD = ➡
        dictionary[@"im:price"][@"attributes"] ➡
        [@"amount"];

        return item;
}

@end
```

In the preceding code for the Network Controller, there are a few different methods that handle important networking tasks. Here's what each of those methods do.

- `retrieveTopSong`: calls the `retrieveJSONFeedWithCompletionHandler:forNumberOfItems:`, passing in a value of 1 for the number of items. This method will be used when creating a complication in Chapter 7 (Building Complications with ClockKit).
- `retrieveJSONFeedWithCompletionHandler:forNumberOfItems:` This method will call out to the iTunes servers for the endpoint that returns a list of top songs in the store, and will set the limit so the requested number of items are returned. The `completionHandler` code block will be executed on error or whenever an NSArray of JSONItems is available. This method is responsible for constructing each `JSONItem` for each song in the returned JSON feed as well. This data is not persisted; therefore each call to this method on the `NetworkController` will provide live data from the server. When iterating through the `NSDictionary` items in the returned feed, the code properly matches the feed attribute to the property in the `JSONItem` class.

Creating the Master-Detail View Controllers

The Master View Controller will be responsible for displaying the Top 10 songs from the JSON feed inside of a `UITableView` implementation.

Begin configuring this master view using the sample code below for MasterViewController.m.

```
@interface MasterViewController ()

@property (nonatomic, strong) NSArray *objects;

@end

@implementation MasterViewController

- (void)viewDidLoad
{
    self.title = @"Top 10 Tunes";
    [self reloadContent:self];
}

#pragma mark - Segues
- (void)prepareForSegue: ➡
(UIStoryboardSegue *)segue sender:(id)sender
{
    if ([[segue identifier] ➡
    isEqualToString:@"showDetail"]) {
        NSIndexPath *indexPath = ➡
        [self.tableView indexPathForSelectedRow];

        JSONItem *detailItem = ➡
        [self.objects ➡
         objectAtIndex:indexPath.row];

        DetailViewController ➡
```

```objc
        *detailController =
        (DetailViewController *)[[[segue
        destinationViewController]
        viewControllers] firstObject];

        [detailController
        setDetailItem:detailItem];
    }
}

#pragma mark - Actions

- (IBAction)reloadContent:(id)sender
{
    [[NetworkController
    sharedNetworkController]
    retrieveJSONFeedWithCompletionHandler:
    ^(NSError *error, NSArray *objects) {

        if (!error && objects) {
            self.objects = objects;

            dispatch_async
            (dispatch_get_main_queue(), ^{
                [self.tableView reloadData];
            });
        }
    } forNumberOfItems:10];
}

#pragma mark - Table View

- (NSInteger)numberOfSectionsInTableView:
(UITableView *)tableView
{
    return 1;
}
```

```objc
- (NSInteger)tableView:(UITableView *)tableView
numberOfRowsInSection:(NSInteger)section
{
    return [self.objects count];
}

- (UITableViewCell *)tableView:
(UITableView *)tableView cellForRowAtIndexPath:
(NSIndexPath *)indexPath
{
    JSONItem *item =
    [self.objects objectAtIndex:indexPath.row];

    UITableViewCell *cell =
    [tableView
    dequeueReusableCellWithIdentifier:@"Cell"
    forIndexPath:indexPath];

    cell.textLabel.text =
    [NSString stringWithFormat:@"%ld - %@",
    (long)indexPath.row + 1, item.songTitle];

    return cell;
}
```

The code that was just added to the project is responsible for populating the Master View Controller `UITableView` with standard `UITableViewCell` objects that will display the top 10 iTunes songs, ranked by popularity.

To complete this view, open the Main.storyboard file, add a `UIBarButtonItem` to the navigation bar, and then connect the button to the `IBAction` named `reloadContent`.

Next, add the following property declaration in `DetailViewController` header file to configure the displayed `JSONItem` object.

```
@property (nonatomic, strong) JSONItem ➡
*detailItem;
```

The following sample code shows the implementation file for the `DetailViewController`. Ensure the code is added to DetailViewController.m.

```
@interface DetailViewController ()
@property (nonatomic, weak) IBOutlet UILabel ➡
*songTitleLabel;

@property (nonatomic, weak) IBOutlet UILabel ➡
*artistTitleLabel;

@property (nonatomic, weak) IBOutlet UILabel ➡
*releaseDateLabel;

@property (nonatomic, weak) IBOutlet UILabel ➡
*albumLabel;

@property (nonatomic, weak) IBOutlet UILabel ➡
*genreNameLabel

@property (nonatomic, weak) IBOutlet UILabel ➡
*priceLabel;

@end

@implementation DetailViewController

- (void)setDetailItem:(id)newDetailItem
{
    if (_detailItem != newDetailItem) {
        _detailItem = newDetailItem;
```

```objc
        [self configureView];
    }
}

- (void)configureView
{
    if (self.detailItem)
    {
        self.title = self.detailItem.songTitle

        self.songTitleLabel.text = ⇒
        self.detailItem.songTitle;

        self.artistTitleLabel.text = ⇒
          self.detailItem.artistName;

        self.releaseDateLabel.text = ⇒
        self.detailItem.releaseDate;

        self.albumLabel.text = ⇒
        self.detailItem.albumName;

        self.genreNameLabel.text = ⇒
        self.detailItem.genreTitle;

        self.priceLabel.text = ⇒
        [NSString stringWithFormat:@"$%.2f", ⇒
        [self.detailItem. priceInUSD floatValue]];
    }
}

- (void)viewDidLoad
{
    [super viewDidLoad];
    [self configureView];
}
```

This Detail View Controller displays the details about a song (song title, artist name, genre, etc) when tapping on a song title in the

Master View Controller, using a Storyboard segue to the DetailViewController.

To finish configuring the detail view, open the Storyboard file and select the Detail View Controller scene. From the Object Library, drag out 12 `UILabel` objects and place them in the detail controller so that it appears like Figure A1.1.

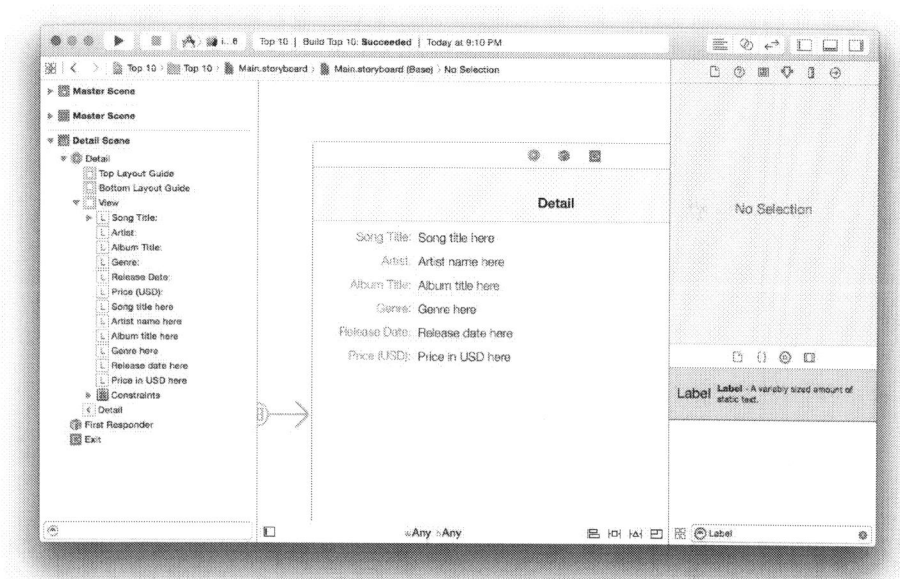

Figure A1.1 – The labels in the detail view are configured using Helvetica Neue Light 15 point font. The header labels are right aligned, and the content labels are left aligned. Auto Layout constraints have been applied to ensure proper alignment when the app is running on a device.

After the labels have been added into the Storyboard view, connect the `IBOutlets` to the labels in the view using the standard Control + Click and drag method from the Detail controller to the appropriate labels in the Storyboard scene.

Creating the WatchKit App Target

A WatchKit app is essentially an iOS Extension target that is copied to and runs on the Apple Watch. This single extension manages the WatchKit app and actionable notifications.

In order to add Apple Watch functionality to the project, a new WatchKit target needs to be created. The following steps can be used to create this new target in the project.

1. Click the project name in the Xcode Project Navigator sidebar
2. Show the project and targets list
3. Select the + button at the bottom of the project and targets list
4. Select watchOS | WatchKit App from the template chooser
5. In the target options dialog that appears when clicking next (Figure A1.2), and checking the option for "Include Complication." Ensure the "Embed in Companion Application" is the iOS app.

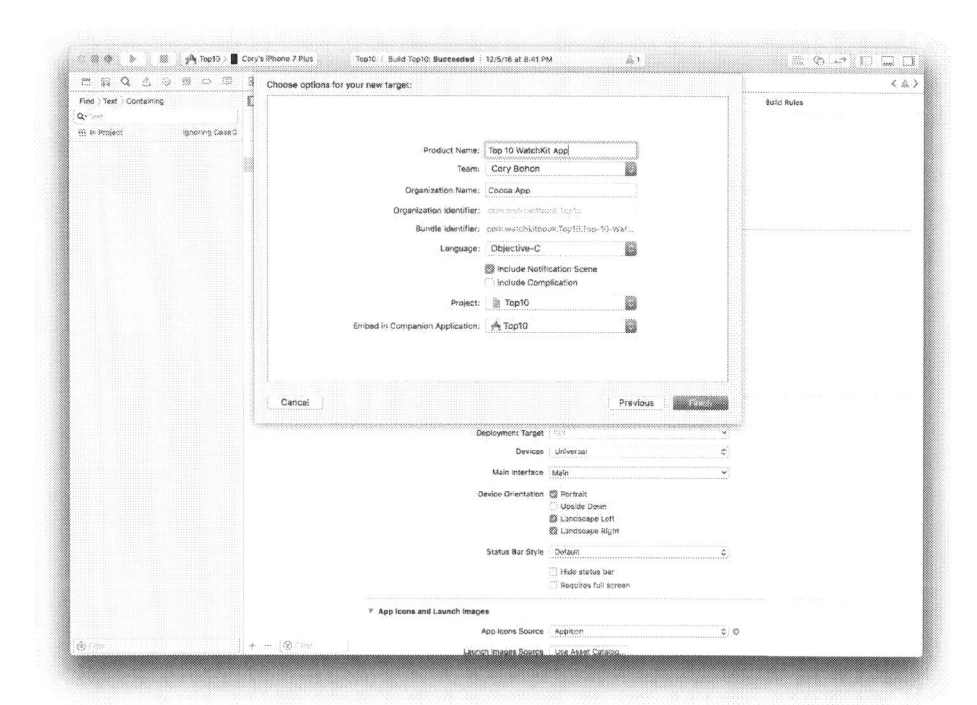

Figure A1.2 - The "Embed in Companion Application" should always be the one that is being submitted to the iTunes App Store since WatchKit apps cannot exist on their own.

Two new groups are created in the project when the target is added: One for the "WatchKit App" and one for the "WatchKit Extension." The WatchKit App folder contains the WatchKit Storyboard and an Xcode asset file for storing images. The WatchKit Extension folder contains the interface and notification controller subclasses. When a new subclass gets created for the Apple Watch implementation, it will be placed in the Extension.

Hello, WatchKit

Throughout the topic chapters in this publication, this sample project will be built upon and additional technologies added as they are taught in the chapters. Until that point, however, add a simple label to the newly created WatchKit target so that it can display something when the app is run inside of the watchOS simulator or on a device.

Do this by opening the Storyboard file created for the watch target called "Interface.storyboard." This Storyboard file is located inside of the WatchKit App group in the Project Explorer.

Once opened, locate the Interface Controller Scene, then drag and drop a Label from the Object Library onto this scene in the Storyboard. Rename the label "Hello, World!" (Figure A1.3).

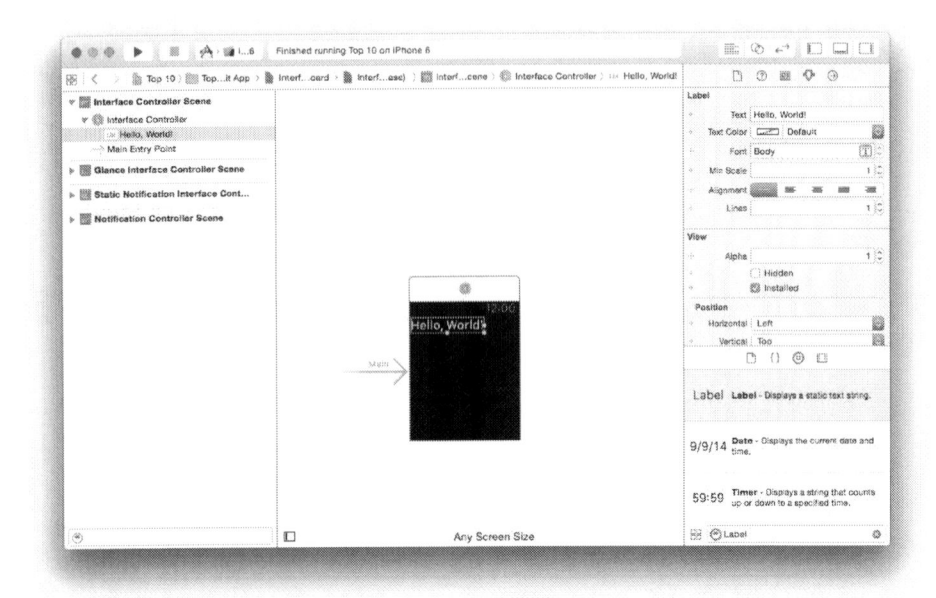

Figure A1.3 – The initial Storyboard scene in a new WatchKit app is called "Interface Controller Scene." This is the first view controller that executes when running the app.

Once the label has been added, select the "WatchKit App" scheme in the Xcode toolbar, then Build & Run the app. Both the iOS simulator and the watch simulator will load and appear in macOS, and after a few seconds, the new watchOS app will spring to life in the Apple Watch simulator window.

Summary

In this appendix, you were able to build out the base iOS and WatchKit app that will be used in this publication to teach examples in each of the topic-specific chapters. This base implementation includes the necessary networking code to pull the top songs feed from the US iTunes store and to display the top 10 songs in the sample iOS app. Finally, you added a WatchKit target to the app and learned how to run the newly added watchOS target in the watchOS simulator on the Mac.

Printed in Great Britain
by Amazon